American Mosaic

Church Planting in Ethnic America

Oscar I. Romo

*A*MERICAN MOSAIC

Church Planting in ETHNIC AMERICA

BROADMAN PRESS
NASHVILLE, TENNESSEE

©Copyright 1993 • Broadman Press

4260-70
ISBN: 0-8054-6070-5

Dewey Decimal Classification: 254.1
Subject Heading: NEW CHURCHES//CHURCH PLANTING//
ETHNIC CHURCHES
Library of Congress Card Catalog Number: 92-41691
Printed in the United States of America

Unless otherwise stated, all Scripture quotations are from the *King James Version of the Bible.*

Scripture quotations marked GNB are from the *Good News Bible:* the Bible in Today's English Version. Old Testament: Copyright ©American Bible Society 1976; New Testament: Copyright ©American Bible Society 1966, 1971, 1976. Used by permission.

Scripture quotations marked RSV are from the *Revised Standard Version of the Bible,* copyright 1946, 1952, ©1971, 1973 by the National Council of Churches in the U.S.A., and used by permission. Scripture quotations marked NASB are from the *New American Standard Bible.* ©The Lockman Foundation, 1960, 1962, 1963, 1968, 1971, 1972, 1973, 1975, 1977. Used by permission.

Library of Congress Cataloging-in-Publication Data

Romo, Oscar I.
    American mosaic : church planting in ethnic America / by Oscar
I. Romo.
        p.   cm.
    ISBN 0-8054-6070-5 :
    1. Church work with minorities—United States.   2. Church
development, New—Baptists.   3. Church growth—Baptists.
4. Minorities—United States.   I. Title.
BV4468.R66   1993
254'.1'08693—dc20
                                                        92-41691
                                                        CIP

To Zoe H. Romo
*faithful companion
for over thirty-five years*

Preface

This book seeks to share experiences acquired during more than forty years of ministry. It is an effort to provide an overview of a national strategy with local applications.

Pastors, missionaries, and numerous other people made the contents of the book relevant among ethnic groups among whom they work. The staff, especially José A. Hernandez, Jaime Prieto, and M. Rodney Webb, provided input and suggestions in the development of the material. W. David Terry assisted with the statistics and prepared the charts.

Several contributed to the preparation of the book. Lyra Crapps compiled materials and proofread the manuscript. Janice Trusty edited as well as proofread the materials. Merry E. Purvis, executive assistant, provided leadership, prepared, and proofread the final manuscript.

My family—wife, Zoe, and children, Miriam R. Reynolds and Nelson O. Romo—provided encouragement and support through the years and in the development of the manuscript.

Oscar I. Romo

Contents

Foreword

Southern Baptists are the most culturally pluralistic denomination in the United States because for many decades their Home Mission Board has had a biblically sound, culturally sensitive approach to reach ethnic groups with the gospel, to establish ethnic congregations, and to train ethnic leaders. A significant factor in the development and implementation of this strategy has been the leadership of Dr. Oscar Romo. Having served as pastor of Hispanic congregations, Associate Director of Language Missions in the Baptist General Convention of Texas, and as Director of the Home Mission Board's Language Church Extension Division, Dr. Romo has accumulated valuable experience.

Dr. Romo shares some of the most important elements of his rich experience in this book. In it he discusses key biblical principles which have undergirded his approach throughout the years. Some of the creative ways in which personnel have been deployed to maximize outreach and church-starting efforts are also shared in this book. The "catalytic missionary" category is one example of this. This book also provides valuable information regarding the development of strategies employed at the local church, association, state convention, and national levels.

Dr. Romo has an earned B.A. degree from Howard Payne University, a divinity degree from Southwestern Baptist Theological Seminary, and a doctorate from Austin Presbyterian Theological Seminary. He has an honorary doctorate from HPU and has received three other honorary doctorates as well.

Romo is the first ethnic to be elected to an administrative and program responsibility in the Southern Baptist Convention. A renowned national and international missiologist who has served as pastor in Brady, Littlefield, and Forth Worth, Texas, Romo provides leadership to over 7,000 congregations among 101 ethnic groups and 97 American Indian tribes that study the Bible in 98 languages throughout the United States and its territories. His leadership has influenced every Southern Baptist agency, as well as other denominations.

The valuable information contained in this book should be of practical value to pastors, denominational leaders, and professors and students in educational institutions. We are truly grateful to Dr. Romo, "Mr. Ethnic Missions," for sharing his insights in this outstanding book.

Daniel R. Sanchez
Professor of Missions
Southwestern Baptist Theological Seminary

Prologue:
Lest We Forget

"Give me your tired, your poor," were empty words to the Chinese and Japanese, the first excluded from U.S. immigration.

Starting in 1917, an immigrant had to be able to read. In 1920, quotas were set for practically every race. It took more than fifty years to change the immigration law and polish the tarnish from "the golden door." The reason for the delay—we forgot where we came from—somewhere else, not here. And we forgot that the strong backs of those who came from across the oceans built America. They lived in tenements that quite exceeded in hopelessness anything we call poverty today.

"But hopelessness isn't quite the right word. Maybe hope is the one thing they did have, if not for themselves, then for their children. We are their children, and since we can't remember the flies, the crowding, the sickness and the dirt, we at least ought to remember that people from somewhere else made this country for us."[1]

Recently a national radio commentator argued that anyone who does not speak English could never be a good American citizen. He said that he didn't believe non-English speaking people should be allowed to vote.

This man's attitude displayed a frightening ignorance of the nature of the American system, both in its present expression and in its historical development.

In the first place, very few Americans—probably only first-generation immigrants from Great Britain—speak English. Most of America's people speak a form of new English we more properly might call "Americanism." It is a blend of a variety of languages, influenced in numerous ways by immigrants who come to our shores. If you don't believe Americanism is distinct from English, ask an Englishman.

Second, probably no other nation in the world has as many foreign-language newspapers and radio/TV broadcasts as does the United States. It is quite possible for individuals to live their entire lives, keep well abreast of current events, and participate actively in the political/economic/social environment of the United States, and never learn to speak English. In fact, if we in the Language Church Extension Division of the Home Mission Board (HMB) have our way, the non-English-speaking Americans will have equal opportunities to worship in the linguistic and cultural context most familiar to them. However, that opportunity may not come if we do not quickly correct some misinformation surfacing in the Southern Baptist Convention. There seems to be a movement to distort a basic concept first applied in our language missions efforts more than twenty-five years ago. This is the multiethnic, yet indigenous, church structure in the midst of a multiethnic culture.

Our basic philosophy is that Southern Baptists should recognize needs of other Baptists to be themselves and, therefore, provide opportunities for their expression of ancestral language and culture. For ethnic Baptists, this recognition includes a willingness on the part of the predominant cultural group (i.e., Anglos) to allow ethnics the privilege of using their native languages, in an appropriate cultural context, to discover the reality of Jesus Christ and to worship God. The idea is not to create a single, homogeneous culture, but to allow culture to set the agenda for our sharing the love of Jesus Christ with all people.

Within this understanding, it is possible for Anglo congregations to open their facilities to people of different ethnic/ language-culture backgrounds.

The plan does not call for assimilation or integration. It does not Americanize ethnics. Nor does it squeeze from them their last drop of ethnic identity or distill from them their last ounce of ethnic pride. Instead, the goal is to recognize that within the wholeness of Jesus Christ, people of various and divergent backgrounds can exist side by side. They can share the same buildings, each group using their unique characteristics, each exercising their God-given abilities, in the manner most effective for missions and ministry. This is not to imply that we encourage segregated churches in the sense of exclusiveness. Quite the contrary, ours is an effort to provide worship most satisfying to the individual. If a black or Hungarian or Korean feels most comfortable worshiping God in a Spanish-language context, that is his/her prerogative.

Although I have visited hundreds of language churches that held services in languages I do not understand, I always felt the sense of oneness that comes in the bond of Jesus Christ. I have spoken English since childhood and exist in an English-speaking environment. Yet for me, there is still a special spiritual significance in worshiping in a Spanish-speaking church. It is the cultural wellspring of my heritage and my thought patterns; it is irreplaceable as a source of my personhood.

This is what the Language Church Extension Division seeks for others. As a result of our efforts, each Sunday Southern Baptists worship God in ninety-eight different languages and numerous American Indian dialects. A Southern Baptist estimate indicates that within the next twenty years, the number of Spanish-speaking Southern Baptists will leap from 150,000 to 300,000; and the number of Korean language Southern Baptist Convention (SBC) churches will triple, from 321 to 1,000.

Without the Home Mission Board's language missions policy, we would never have been able to take advantage of the groundwork laid by foreign missionaries to make such inroads into the Indonesian refugee community which immigrated to our shores. Nor would there be nearly so great an opportunity to share Christ with the internationals who daily come to the United States—and who, in decades ahead, may prove the most important "missionary force" available to Southern Baptists.

All Southern Baptist accomplishments among ethnics have been because we practiced a policy of language missions that attempts to recognize America as a mosaic of unmelted people. These people, unmelted ethnics—those who keep their cultural and language identities—are equally American as any Anglo from London. It would be well for us, as we continue to move through the 1990s, to remember once again that the United States is a nation of immigrants, a tapestry of cultures and traditions and languages. Americans must respect this heritage and build on it; for in so doing, we will not only create a stronger Southern Baptist Convention but will also come closer to building the true multiethnic kingdom of God on earth.

Note

1. Charles Kuralt, *Dateline America,* (New York: Harcourt, Brace, and Jovanovich, 1979), 25-26.

1 Toward a Philosophy of Ethnic Missions

A philosophy of Language Missions has gradually emerged throughout the past forty years. During these years, the author has been committed to sharing the gospel among ethnics in America, experiencing frustration in imposing programs that often did not meet the needs of the people and created a financial burden on them. Although done without intent, these programs gave more emphasis to acculturation than to evangelization.

The years have been ones of experimentation in adaptations and/or developing various approaches of helping the people mature in their Christian life-styles. Those experiences indicated that the gospel could be shared within the cultural context of the various ethnic groups that comprise the American mosaic.

A Theological Basis

The United States is often called a melting pot. This concept seeks to submerge new Americans and minority ethnic groups into the American way of life, resulting in their losing their unique self-identities and heritages. Yet the search for identity, desire to achieve, and the right of ethnic Americans to be themselves have brought about the acknowledgment that our nation is indeed a pluralistic society.

A pluralistic society is defined as an aggregation of peoples of different groups characterized by their heritages, cultures, languages, and life-styles. Ethnic America conforms to this definition. Therefore, any appropriate missions endeavor must take into account the multilingual, multicultural dimensions of the society.

Those who genuinely seek to respond to the God of Abraham, Isaac, and Jacob are conscious of pluralism and desire to minister and witness in that context.

The following are some of the theological premises essential for missions in a pluralistic context.

Belief in a Triune God

A thorough understanding of God's revealed goals for missions includes the revelation of the will of the Father, the lordship of Christ, and the work of the Holy Spirit. (Gen. 1:1-2; 2:7; 18:1ff; Ex. 3:14; 6:2-3; Ps. 2:7ff; 110:1ff; Isa. 7:14; Job 26:13; Matt. 1:18-23; 3:16-17; 4:1; 6:9ff; 7:11; 8:29; 12:28-32; 23:9; 28:19; Mark 1:10, 12; Luke 1:35; 4:1, 18-19.)

Belief in God's Love for All People

Love, defined as the self-imparting quality in the divine nature, leads God to seek the highest good and most complete possession of His creatures. God created all men equal and extends His love equally to all regardless of racial, linguistic, ethnic, or social distinctions. Love in its ultimate form seeks a relation with intelligent, moral, and free beings. God's love seeks to awaken persons to return His love. Love in its purest form calls for a complete and unrestrained self-giving and the complete possession of each by the other. (Ex. 34:6-7; Ps. 18:20-22; 33:5; 83:18; 119:64; 145:7-9; Is. 45; 61:11; Gen. 12:3; 1 Kings 18:39; Rom. 8:28-39; John 1:12-14.)

Belief in the Lostness of Mankind

People are unable to save themselves. They need God's saving grace. They are lost because of their inherited nature.

Sin weakens and depraves people's nature, the very element and faculty of their beings. Body, soul, and spirit are under its power. Their minds are darkened, their hearts depraved, and their wills perverted by sin. Without divine help, sin defeats them. (Rom. 3:23; 6:23; Ps. 51:5; Jer. 17:9; Eph. 2:3.)

Belief that All People Must Come to Jesus Christ

One religion is not as good as another. Truth has become objectively real and binding in Jesus. Jesus reveals the relationship that exists between God and mankind and among persons. He restores those relationships as no one else can. In Jesus, mankind finds not only God but also his own identity in and beyond culture. (Gen. 3:15; Ex. 3:14-17; Matt. 1:21; 4:17; Luke 1:68-69; 19:10; John 1:11-14; Acts 4:12.)

Belief About the Nature and Functions of a Local Church

God's covenants with His people have always placed upon them the responsibility for sharing His love and nature. The exiled prophet, Isaiah, recognized this best when he proclaimed God's people to be a light to the Gentiles (nations). The people of God today, the church, have the same responsibilities in an equally pluralistic setting.

A church is a congregation of baptized believers who live in the reconciling love of God. Christ is the common bond for these believers. The church as the body of Christ seeks to carry out the Great Commission to proclaim, worship, educate, and minister to the ends of the earth. (Is. 2:1-4; 42:6; 49:6; 1 John 3:1; 4:10-11; 1 Cor. 12:27; Eph. 4:16; John 4:23-24; Acts 1:8; Matt. 11:29; 20:26-28.)

Belief of Unity and Diversity of the Body of Christ

All Christians are "baptized into Christ's body." All Christians receive one or more spiritual gifts that determine what functions they should have in the body—the church. Jesus

Christ is the head of the body, and every member functions properly by using his or her spiritual gift(s) in cooperation with other members' gifts.

The body of Christ functions properly when all gifts are in use through the power of God's Spirit. The body of Christ is universal, with many local manifestations. Certain spiritual gifts may or may not exist in any particular part of the body. Spiritual gifts should not produce pride or envy. They should help people share the good news with others within their cultural context. (1 Cor. 7:7; 12:1; 13;3; Rom. 12: Eph. 4.)

Missions in Context

God created humans in His image. However, mankind developed cultural differences almost from the beginning. Cain was a farmer. Abel was a rancher. The farmer and the rancher saw life from different perspectives and evidently worshiped God in different ways.

The story of the Tower of Babel (see Gen. 11:1-9) is important for a theology that considers both our common humanity as creatures of God and the manifold pluralism in the Creator's purpose. The story portrays a clash of human and divine wills, of centripetal and centrifugal forces. "Surprisingly, it is the human beings who strive to maintain a primeval unity, based on one language, a central living space, and a single aim. It is God who counteracts the movement toward a center with a centrifugal force that disperses them into linguistic, spatial, and ethnic diversity."[1]

"By counting the people enumerated in Genesis 10, the rabbis later figured at 72 the number (of languages) spoken in the Ancient World."[2] The ancient world was multilingual.

The Old Testament

The Promises to Abram

Two thousand years before Christ, God called Abram to leave his home, his business, and his relatives. The call had a purpose: to make him the head of a new people by which God would reveal Himself to the rest of the world. Promises made to Abram included responsibilities. "I will make of thee a great nation" (Gen. 12:2). This promise was a source of happiness and a test of faith. Abram had no children; he and his wife were old, and Sarah was barren. But faith has a way of overcoming doubt and unbelief. "Great nation" means more than a heavily populated land. The great influence of monotheism made Israel unique.

The promise, "In thee shall all families of the earth be blessed" (v. 3), gave this Chaldean man the assurance that his seed would be a source of blessedness for all people of the earth.

Israel was God's people. They were His more by redemption than by creation. As Moses said, "Happy art thou, O Israel: who is like unto thee, O people saved by the Lord, the shield of thy help, and who is the sword of thy excellency!" (Deut. 33:29)! They also are His by discipline: "But the Lord hath taken you, and brought you forth out of the iron furnace, even out of Egypt, to be unto him a people of inheritance, as ye are this day" (4:20). Mainly, they were His for a special mission—being the medium of God's self-revelation to the rest of the nations and being the people from whose midst the Messiah would come. They were to be the carriers and role models of a message of love for the entire world.

The Message of the Psalms

The Psalms have a ring of universality: the knowledge of God through Israel's mediation shall bring together the nations—the peoples, *ta ethne*—to worship the only God of both the ethnic and the Israelite. Our Bible versions use the word "people" (Ps. 57:9), which the Septuagint translates *ta ethne*—"the nations."

Psalm 67, a harvest prayer that all people may worship God, emphasizes that God's mercy and salvation may be known among the nations. The whole earth, Hebrew and ethnic, is included in this prayer.

Paul quoted Psalm 117 in Romans 15:11. About this, Spurgeon said: "In vain might the prophet invite the Gentiles to praise Jehovah unless they were to be gathered into the unity of the faith together with the children of Abraham."[3] This exhortation to the Gentiles to praise Jehovah is proof that the spirit of the Old Testament differs widely from the narrow views of the Jews in Jesus' time. God's grace and mercy were not circumscribed to Israel only, but were the patrimony of all the races and peoples of the earth.

The Providence of a Translation

During the exile, changes occurred among the Jews of Babylonia and Persia. The language spoken by them was no longer Hebrew but Aramaic. Hebrew became the language of students and of the synagogue. Therefore, an interpreter had to translate Scriptures read in public services.

Jews of the West faced the same problem. Children of Hebrew families were more and more under the influence of Hellenism; the Scriptures were not being read and studied. Hence, a need existed to translate the Scriptures from Hebrew to Greek.

Jewish translators, under the patronage of Ptolemy Philadelphus, translated the Pentateuch. When preachers went out to fulfill the Great Commission, they could speak freely to everybody in the *lingua franca* of their day and make use of the providential translation called the Septuagint.

The New Testament

The Example of Jesus

When we speak about Christianity and its gospel, we must talk about ethnic/language-culture missions. In a world profoundly fragmented by all kinds of conflicts—social, economic, political, racial—Jesus Christ ministered, taught, healed, preached, and comforted people. His apostles were ordinary people. His disciples came from all walks of life. Publicans were His friends and even harlots looked at Him with love.

Some of His most beautiful praises were for members of despised ethnic groups. He spoke directly to a Roman centurion whose faith He highly praised (Luke 7:1-10), to a Samaritan woman whom He led to a spontaneous confession of sin and repentance (John 4), to a Syrophenician woman (Mark 7:26), and to two Roman officers, including Pilate (John 18:33-38). He neglected no race or ethnic group.

What language did he use with that great diversity of people? He must have been at least a bilingual man, at home in Aramaic (the common Palestinian tongue) and Greek (the universal language of His day spoken by the Gentiles). Sometimes we have intimations of His sayings. Even on the cross, we hear Him exclaiming, "Eli, Eli, lama sabachthani" (Matt. 27:46). The Roman government attempted to reach all people as they wrote on the cross above His head the cause of Jesus in three languages: Hebrew, Greek, and Latin.

Birth of Language Missions

Before ascending into heaven, Jesus commanded His disciples to stay in Jerusalem until the power of the Holy Spirit came upon them (Luke 24:49). Only then would they be qualified to become His "martyrs"—His witnesses. So eleven Christians waited in prayer and supplication. On the Day of Pentecost, they were filled with the Holy Spirit and "began to speak, . . . as the Spirit gave them utterance" (Acts 2:4). Jewish men, "devout men, out of every nation under heaven. . . . were confounded, because every man heard them speak in his own language. . . . saying one to another . . . how hear we every man in our own tongue, wherein we were born?" (vv. 5-8). Ethnic/language-culture missions were born!

Breaking of the Old Wall

The church of Jerusalem was reluctant to go into an ethnic world. Their Jewish proclivities were strong and kept them orbiting the temple. They observed the prescribed hours of prayer, fulfilled some vows according to the Mosaic system, and abstained from some food. Their roots were so deep that some traveled to other towns with a tendency to make Christianity a sect of Judaism.

The wall of separation, however, began to show the first signs of cracking. Philip went to Samaria where the people's response was the fulfillment of any preacher's dream. The success was so notable that the church of Jerusalem sent Peter and John to Samaria. Luke says, "And when they had testified and preached the word of the Lord, they returned to Jerusalem, and preached the gospel in many villages of the Samaritans" (8:25).

Another crack of the wall was Peter's visit with the Roman centurion, Cornelius. Peter was the one who, in an official manner, went over the wall into the Gentile yard. He did not go on his own volition, but he did go. And he declared, "Ye know how that it is an unlawful thing for a man that is a Jew to keep company, or come unto one of another nation; but God hath shewed me that I should not call any man common or unclean" (10:28).

Before Peter could complete his sermon, the Spirit fell upon those who heard the word. Jews and Gentiles alike received the gift of the Holy Spirit.

Paul, Apostle to the Gentiles

Paul was a bicultural, bilingual man from an ethnic minority. Before his conversion, he had been a Jew and continued to be one, but he was also a Hellenistic Jew. A Jesuit author, Ferdinand Prat, states that Paul was familiar with the Bible in two languages, but he almost always quoted it in Greek, perhaps because, as he was writing in Greek, the Septuagint came to his mind more spontaneously. Prat observed: "According to calculations subject to revision, out of eighty-four quotations, thirty-four reproduce exactly the text of the Seventy, thirty-six depart from it very little, ten offer notable differences, and two are given according to the Hebrew text."[4]

After his work in Cyprus, Saul's name was changed to Paul (13:9). From then on, he spoke to members of two ethnic groups.

Finally, while a prisoner of Caesar, Paul used Greek to evangelize those of the "household of Caesar" (Phil. 4:22).

Testimony of Translations

The first translation of the Hebrew Scriptures into Greek, the Septuagint, came as an answer to a great need experienced by an ethnic group losing a facet of its ethnicity—its home language. They could not help the change. Hence, the pioneering translation.

Many years later, as the gospel began to be preached in every land, communication became a problem. For that reason, missionaries learned the language or dialect of a group or a nation. Their knowledge helped carry the message of God to ethnic groups. Since then, hundreds of versions and translations have multiplied their testimony—that teaching the gospel means using the other person's language if Jesus' message is to be understood and accepted. The gospel must be communicated to people everywhere in the language of their souls.[5]

Missions in Ethnic America

Americans inherited language and cultural values of their forefathers—a wealth unique to our country, a nation of immigrants. Beckoned by Cape Cod, the pilgrims came seeking religious freedom. Puritans and others followed. America, where a free man could own property and worship as dictated by his soul, became a laboratory of freedom for the world.

Millions of people in our nation, excluding African-Americans, identify themselves as belonging to an ethnic/language-culture group.[6] These invisible, as well as visible, ethnics live throughout the country. Urban areas have a high ethnic density. The greatest percentage of growth in ethnicity is in the South.[7] Ethnics touch every fiber of our lives. They are involved in music, arts, law, medicine, science, education, and politics.

Ethnolinguistic America

The new world discovered by Columbus was inhabited by people whose cultural, linguistic, scientific, and religious lives can be seen as superior to the continent from which Columbus departed on his historical adventure. "The peopling of America is one of the great dramas of human history."[8] America's cultural history is a bundle of paradoxes. Americans are of mixed origins. Yet, we are one people.

The land that receives the world's tired, poor, huddled masses that yearn to breathe free has become the "American mosaic," reflecting diversities of cultural and linguistic values.

The wide spectrum of America's true character is "that we are a common culture which is composed of diverse cultures."[9] Most Americans acknowledge the multicultural concept. Their acceptance of these concepts permits people to live in various phases of the chromatic scale of assimilation, becoming multilingual and multicultural. Yet they retain their cultural identities.

America is not only a nation of immigrants, but also of foundlings tossed on the doorstep of a strong country; thrown into the melting pot with Europeans, American Indians, Hispanics, Arabs, Asians, and others. Bleaching of the nation has proven that Americans, although encouraged and often forced to assimilate, retain their visible identities, as well as their cultural and linguistic heritages.

America faces the crisis of a still-emerging nationhood with a puzzle of cultural diversities. The uniqueness of its texture indicates, according to Gordon Wood of Brown University, that to be an American is to *believe* in certain things, not to *be* certain things.

Language and culture are a vital part of a person's heritage. This heritage permits diverse ethnic, racial, religious, and social aspects to exist as autonomous components within the confines of a common way of life—a life in a pluralistic society unique to the American heritage.[10]

The linguistic dimensions of the world are classified into 5,000 speech communities. Some communities have millions of members; others have fewer than a thousand members. Through the linguistic patterns, people express their joy, love, and hate, as well as share and acquire knowledge. Dimensions of these patterns symbolize unity, understanding, and misunderstanding in the terminology, type, meaning, significance, and accent. These patterns uphold values, premises, beliefs, opinions, and the meaning of life in keeping with acquired cultural experiences.[11]

The gospel must be communicated in the hearer's cultural context and in a language common to his or her understanding. Wycliffe Bible translators have said that individuals are never effectively reached with the gospel until reached in the language of their souls. Missiologist and translator, Dr. Eugene Nida, said that when people learn to love and hate in a language, it is that language in which the gospel can best be communicated. Effective communication comes by recognizing the importance of language and culture.

American life-styles are comparable to the chromatic scale in music. Harmony occurs when notes are utilized in proper relationship to each other. It is impossible to write a harmonious song with just one note. Sharps and flats, major and minor keys, time and quality of intonations, as well as rests, provide harmony, rhythm, and beauty.[12] Linguistic rhythms and intonations of the 636 languages and numerous dialects used to communicate by America's 500 ethnic groups make possible the composition, "America the Beautiful."

American Indians

Hundreds of years before Columbus discovered America, Indians migrated from Siberia to the New World. Indian forefathers, who varied in physical appearance, customs, and language, greeted the settlers at Plymouth Rock.[13]

Indian dialects can be heard today in urban centers such as Boston, Los Angeles, Chicago, Dallas, and New York. These Americans, representing 497 tribes speaking 250 languages and dialects, are more numerous in urban cities than on reservations.

Pride is a cultural heritage that teaches Indians to live in harmony with nature and each other. Time is measured on a living-here-and-now basis. Indians highly value integrity, individuality, and concern for each other. United by their culture, American Indians try to retain their identities and languages. It is this cultural heritage that "makes possible a channel for relationship in the great urban areas of the nation."[14]

Arabs

People from the Arab world began to immigrate to the United States in the latter part of the nineteenth century. They came to escape persecution, to seek economic stability, an education, to join relatives, or for an adventure. Today large numbers of Arabic people are found in the urban centers of the nation.[15] Detroit is the largest Arabic city outside of the Middle East.

The Arab's assimilation and acculturation varies from one place to another. However, their religious heritage (Islam), tenacity of their language, and their desire for identity permit them to maintain the customs and ideas of their homelands.

Arabic communities are cultural and linguistic rather than

geographical. However, the Arab population—more than 3 million—is gradually developing areas in urban centers.

Cultural values, tenacity of the language and the religious heritage of the Arabic Christians led to the gradual development of Arab Christian communities. Such communities hold no affiliation with a particular denomination. These Christians pray and call for Baptists to "come over into Macedonia, and help us" (Acts 16:9) reach other Arabs with the gospel.

Asians

Asian heritage originated in Asia, south and southeast of the Himalayas.[16]

Chinese people came to America's West Coast soon after the discovery of gold. Their children worked hard to secure an education and establish an economic base. Today they contribute to the life-styles of the nation.

Chinese populations in U.S. cities are increasing. American-born Chinese influence and prosper in education, science, politics, law, and medicine.[17]

No immigrant group encountered more prejudice and discrimination than the Japanese. They faced denial of citizenship, ownership of land, and often complete exclusion. Yet today the increasing influence of the Issei (foreign-born Japanese) and the Nisei (American-born Japanese) can be felt as they become proprietors, exert political influence, and migrate to U.S. cities. Their linguistic tenacity and cultural heritage continue to provide cohesiveness that overcomes legal, social, and employment obstacles.[18]

The tenacity of Asian cultures and languages, such as Korean, Filipino, Thai, and Vietnamese, will continually contribute to the formation and development of American life-styles.

Deaf Persons

Deafness, according to *Webster's New Collegiate Dictionary*, is lacking or deficient in the sense of hearing. People have varying degrees of hearing and deafness, from normal hearing to total deafness. Hard-of-hearing people are those whose hearing is defective but functional with or without hearing aids. Deaf persons are those whose hearing is nonfunctional for ordinary purposes. This includes people born deaf and those whose hearing became nonfunctional later in life due to illness or an accident. Hard-of-hearing people can usually participate in regular church activities. Deaf people need special provisions.

About 1.8 million severely hearing-impaired people live in the United States. They are of all cultures; adults and children, rich, middle-class, and poor; good and bad; well-educated and illiterate. Deaf people are everywhere; rarely will a town be so small as to have no deaf people.

The United States places its deaf-blind population into three general groups: (1) children born deaf or losing hearing early in life and then losing sight, (2) children born blind or becoming blind early in life and then becoming deaf, and (3) children born deaf-blind or becoming deaf-blind during their early years before developing useful means of self-expression. About 70 percent of deaf-blind adults become deaf first and then blind as a result of diseases, heredity, or accidents. They have characteristics of deaf adults of the same age, except they have become blind. They had the same education and employment level as their deaf friends before losing their vision.

Deaf-blind people need communication and mobility. Isolation makes communication their primary need.

No denomination, including the Southern Baptist Convention, has a national program for deaf-blind people. They leave most of the work with deaf-blind people to individual churches and interpreters. As a result, few deaf-blind individuals are reached by churches. The primary ministry will always be one-to-one.

In deaf educational and religious circles there is a program called Total Communication, which encompasses avenues of communication such as sign language, finger spelling, auditory amplification, speech, speech reading, writing, gestures, and reading.[19] Primary communication methods for deaf people are lipreading, writing, and dactylology (sign language). Lipreading is an art. The deaf person able to master it has a greater range of communication. However, few are able to master it fully, and then it is usable only in small groups. Even the most proficient lip-reader cannot read the lips of a preacher in a large sanctuary or on a television screen.

Writing and dactylology are the basic tools of communication for the adult deaf. Because it offers an ease of expression and is adaptable to groups as well as individual communication, dactylology is best suited for use in public meetings such as worship services. Dactylology, as used by the deaf, was brought to the United States from France by Dr. Thomas Hopkins Gallaudet in the early 1800s.

Dactylology is a system of communication through use of fingerspelling, hand signs, facial and body gestures, and pantomime that have come to be recognized by the deaf to represent words and ideas of which their speech is composed. Dactylology, like other languages, has rules of grammar, syntax, and usage. It is a living language and is constantly changing and growing. For the deaf, it is even a satisfactory means of singing.

Deaf persons, because of their unique circumstances, have gradually developed a cultural background. Ministry among deaf people becomes a staggering challenge as the gospel is shared in the language and cultural context of deaf people.

Europeans

Europeans came to the United States seeking life's necessities and freedom. Many came as displaced people, making sacrifices to capture the American dream.[20]

Europeans belong to five basic groups—German, Slavic, Latin, Baltic, and Scandinavian. These invisible ethnics appre-

ciate America but retain their language and cultural uniqueness.

Contributions of European Americans are numerous. A
German immigrant introduced the kindergarten.[21] A French-
born industrialist, Eleuthère Irénée Du Pont, established the
chemical industry. Alexander Graham Bell, a Scottish-born
inventor, gave us the telephone. David Sarnoff, a Russian
immigrant, pioneered in radio. A German physicist, Albert
Einstein, advanced the development of atomic energy. Arturo
Toscanini, an Italian, brought greatness to the American musical world.

Europeans added color and uniqueness to the American
lifestyle. Their cultural heritages gradually wove themselves
into American life.

Hispanics

Hispanic Americans identify with the Spanish language and
culture and may or may not be American citizens. These
people comprise the nation's second largest minority and the
world's fifth largest Spanish-speaking nation.[22]

Hispanics in the United States belong to several distinctive
subcultural groups. Mexican Americans live primarily in the
Southwest, with sizable numbers in northern New Mexico and
Colorado; Puerto Ricans live primarily in the Northeast;
Cubans live primarily in Miami, New York City, and California.
Central and South Americans live throughout America.

Hispanics speak English and Spanish. They can relate to both
English and Spanish cultures. Hispanics are creating a new life-
style that includes the best of both cultures; yet allows them to
retain their identities, cultural heritages, and linguistic tenacities.

Leonard Bernstein once said that the rhythm and color of
Latin American music is almost irresistible. Hispanic-American
musicians Carmen Cavallero, José Iturbi, and Pablo Casals are
but a few of those who have contributed to our musical
enjoyment.

The performing arts have been enriched by José Quintero, José Ferrer, Rita Moreno, Cesar Romero, Ricardo Montalban, and Anthony Quinn, whose sensitivity and emotional capacities helped them portray intimate values that contributed to the American way of life.[23]

Immigrants and Refugees

People around the world view the United States as a land of unlimited opportunities and a veritable utopia. Freedom and the hope of prosperity have brought millions to our shores. Many of these have established residence in this country, with a large number eventually hoping to obtain citizenship.

America is a land of immigrants. Most historians agree that even the "first Americans," American Indians, immigrated to the Western Hemisphere from the Far East. People who legally enter the United States from other countries come in the following classifications:[24]

- Immigrants: those who come on a permanent basis to reside in the United States and who may acquire citizenship
- Nonimmigrants: people in this country on temporary visas
- Refugees: those seeking asylum

Immigrants to the United States include people of all races, cultures, and creeds. They and their ancestors have made America unique among nations.

Opposition to new immigrants began in the mid-nineteenth century. In the latter part of that century, the U.S. Congress passed laws to prevent entry of undesirables, such as convicts and prostitutes. The early twentieth century brought selective immigration laws and a permanent quota law. Over the years, other laws were passed that affected immigrants.

Refugees are individuals, who, because of persecution, oppression, or calamity, left their homelands and are unwilling or unable to return. They represent people from all walks of life. They, like our ancestors, seek a new life of freedom, opportunity, and purpose in America. Refugees are not a new phenomenon.

Soon after the birth of Jesus and immediately after the wise men left, God warned Joseph in a dream, "Arise, and take the young child and his mother, and flee into Egypt, and be thou there until I bring thee word: for Herod will seek the young child to destroy him. When he arose, he took the young child and his mother by night and departed into Egypt: and was there until the death of Herod" (Matt. 2:13-15). Jesus and His parents were refugees.

Refugees have been victims of wars and persecutions from the beginning of civilization. It would appear that never in history have so many fled their homelands, seeking a new life in other countries. The United States has received millions of such people, and their need for a place to begin life again seems greater than ever.[25]

No one wants to be a refugee. The majority of refugees became so as the result of political decision or indecision. Refugees' decisions to leave their homes and seek asylum, with all the pain and courage that involves for them and their families, were their response to something that happened and frightened or repelled them irrevocably.

Tragically, refugees cannot assert any right for themselves in any persuasive way. They become the victims of other people's decisions. Beneath the statistics and arguments that cause and effect, refugees are people—men, women, and children—who eat, breathe, pray, and hope like the rest of us. Their right to our help in their circumstances can only be denied if we deny the God who gave us life and made us brothers to them. By their rootlessness and need, they personify modern human inability to cope with problems in relationships with his fellow-man. We are all part of this story, and gratefully so, because we have learned that we can help with our sympathy, our prayers, and our contributions.[26]

The refugee's saga provides the opportunity to faithfully and generously share the love of Jesus Christ.

Internationals

America, the land of opportunity, attracts people from around the world. Millions who enter as internationals establish a residency that eventually qualifies them for citizenship.

Other millions, however, spend only limited time in this country. Technically, the Immigration and Naturalization Service designates them as nonimmigrants. Having specific time limitations from a few days to several years, these internationals (Home Mission Board designation) range from diplomats and doctors to traders and tourists.

A large number of these come from Mexico, followed by Japan, the United Kingdom, Germany, and France. Asian countries have increased immigration 137 percent during the past decade because of 1965 changes in quota laws.[27]

Internationals will obviously be found in large educational, medical, and governmental complexes, but their locations are by no means restricted to these areas. A remote military installation, industry, state hospital, or port may be a source of contacts. Rare indeed are the sections of the country that cannot conduct some type of specialized international ministry.

Exposure to a different culture frequently creates an openness to previously foreign ideas.[28] Thus, while in the United States, internationals are probably more receptive to the gospel than in their homelands. Openness, coupled with Christian concern, can build bridges to people with needs in a new land.

Finances, the pace of American life, loneliness, and confusion create feelings of despair and hurt. A helping hand and an understanding heart bind wounds and open avenues of witness and ministry.

Many things about the American way of life may be confusing and frustrating to a foreign visitor, just as customs and practices of other cultures may bewilder or offend us. Seeing others as people transcends such cultural peculiarities. Just as cultural differences influence our food, family structure, concept of time, and friends, they influence religious practices and concepts. Our Christian witness, to be genuinely effective, must take these factors into account and not force an international Christian into a peculiarly American mold. The Spirit of Christ is multicultural as well as multilingual.

Understanding principles of intercultural communications makes possible programs of cross-cultural outreach. Often crises develop in the life of a foreign visitor in which alert, caring Christians can assist. A global sensitivity is prerequisite to an effective witness to internationals.

Recognizing the unique and singular nature of the opportunity makes the task even more urgent. Diplomats, students, seamen, and tourists from countries where missionaries can never go, come to our shores daily. Our mission field here can potentially become Christ's missionaries back home. Thus, we have the challenge and responsibility of introducing these people to Jesus Christ. Tact, patience, and love are required in leading a person of another religious background to a saving knowledge of Jesus.

The area of greatest neglect, and possibly greatest opportunity, is the international tourist. Mobile, expectant, anxious, and often non-English-speaking, the international tourist presents an unclaimed challenge to ministry. With numbers expected to double, Christians must respond with creativity, sensitivity, and love.

Diversity Amid Unity

In a sense, America is a modern Tower of Babel. It is a pluralistic society—an aggregation of peoples characterized by different heritages, cultures, languages, and life-styles—dispersed across an entire continent. Ethnic origins of American people are diverse, with new elements constantly being added. "To equate ethnic and foreign is a mistake."[29] In a pluralistic society where more than sixty-six million people in 1989 indicated a non-English language as their mother tongue, plus an estimated twenty-three million Hispanics, the following "three principles provide an important measure of a civilized reconciliation of unity and diversity."[30]

- "In the United States, ethnicity has not been permitted to become an instrument of territorial sovereignty or of political exclusion. . . .
- Individuals are free to make as much or as little of their ethnic belonging as they choose.
- Individuals organize together in voluntary associations. They are encouraged to nourish such sentiments, memories, aspirations, and practices of group life as they choose."[31]

The American concept includes equality for all. "The oath of citizenship does not require the individual to renounce his cultural belonging or cultural heritage."[32] Ethnic America indeed conforms to these dimensions. Therefore, any appropriate missions endeavor must take into account the multilingual, multicultural dimensions of pluralistic America.

If ethnic Americans, who communicate better in a language other than American English, are to acquire a faith in Jesus Christ, it is imperative that it be acknowledged that "faith cometh by hearing and hearing by the word of God" (Rom. 10:17).

The validity of the continually emerging philosophy of ethnic/language-culture missions that has respect for peoples' dignity and responsibility for self-determination under God can best be attested to by the growth and multidimensional approach that constantly seeks to adapt to changes of approach that meet the spiritual and social needs of the people. It also addresses the acceptability and influence in Southern Baptist life, in secular and government organizations. Missiologist C. Peter Wagner wrote, "Today Southern Baptists are probably five to ten years ahead of most other denominations in perceiving the true spiritual needs of Americans who are un-melted."[33]

Notes

1. Andrew M. Greeley and Gregory Baum, *Ethnicity* (New York: Seabury Press, 1977), 63.
2. George A. Buttrick and Keith R. Crim, eds., *The Interpreters Dictionary of the Bible* (Nashville: Abingdon Press, 1954), 67.
3. C.H. Spurgeon, *The Treasury of David* (Mich.: Zondervan Publishing House, 1950), vol. 5, 98.
4. S.J. Ferdinand Prat, *La Teologia de Pablo* (Mexico: Editorial Jus, 1947), vol. 1, 27.
5. Eugene Nida, *Customs and Cultures* (New York: Harper and Brothers, 1954), 222.
6. *America's Ethnicity* (Atlanta: Home Mission Board), 1981, 240.
7. Ibid., 247.
8. Thomas Sowell, *Ethnic America* (New York: Basic Books, Inc., Pub., 1981), 3.
9. F. Michael Novak, *The Rise of the Unmeltable Ethnic* (New York: MacMillan Co.), 1972, 35.
10. Eugene Nida, *Customs and Cultures* (New York: Harper and Brothers, 1954).
11. Eugene Nida, *Message and Mission* (S. Pasadena: William Carey Library, 1972).
12. Oscar I. Romo, "Harmony in America," *The Baptist Program* (Nashville: Executive Committee, SBC, 1975), 20.
13. *Language Missions Manual* (Atlanta: Home Mission Board), unpublished, 150.
14. Stan Steiner, *The New Indian* (New York: Harper and Row, 1968), 187.
15. Yvonne Haddad, "Arabs in America" (Boston: 1974), unpublished paper.
16. B.L. Sung, *Mountain of Gold* (New York: MacMillan, 1967), 4.
17. Ibid., 245.
18. Dennis Ogawa, *Kodomo Notame Ni* (Honolulu: University of Hawaii Press, 1978), 528.
19. Eugene D. Mindel and Vernon McCay, *They Grow in Silence* (Silver Spring: National Association of the Deaf, 1971), 61 ff.
20. Charles H. Mindel and Robert W. Habenstein, *Ethnic Families in America* (New York: Elsevier, 1977), 98.
21. Stephen Thernstorm, *Harvard Encyclopedia of American Ethnic Groups* (Cambridge: Harvard University, Belknap Press, 1980), 420.
22. *Language Missions Manual* (Atlanta: Home Mission Board), 61, unpublished.
23. Ibid., 65.
24. U.S. Congress, *A Report on U.S. Immigration Law and Policy: 1952-1979* (Washington, D.C.: Government Printing Office, 1979).
25. Frederick A. Norwood, *Strangers and Exiles* (Nashville: Abingdon Press, 1969), vol. 2, 369.

26. John George Stoessinger, *The Refugee and the World Community* (Minneapolis: University of Minnesota Press, 1956), 3.

27. *America's Ethnicity* (Atlanta: Home Mission Board, 1979), 246.

28. Philip R. Harris and Robert T. Moran, *Managing Cultural Differences* (Houston: Gulf Publishing Co., 1979), 4.

29. Stephen Thernstorm, *Harvard Encyclopedia of American Ethnic Groups* (Cambridge: Harvard University, Belknap Press, 1980), 11.

30. Ibid., 776.

31. Ibid., 776.

32. Ibid., 777.

33. C. Peter Wagner, *Your Spiritual Gifts Can Help Your Church Grow* (Glendale, Calif.: Regal Books, 1979), 201.

2 Reshaping Global America

"For nearly a century, historians have searched for the wellspring of American politics and culture."[1] America, hardly the "melting pot" described by history texts, has been a land that from its beginning was marked by diversity, not homogeneity. The search by Americans for a cultural identity has shattered the myth that America has evolved into one homogenous mass culture that uses American English as the language of all the people. Although Americans share many aspects of life (e.g., fast foods, television programs, etc.), we remain a diverse nation.

The last part of the twentieth century has brought about a change in American attitudes toward ethnicity. In many instances, it has created a desire for almost everyone to have and/or seek an identity. Ethnic pride, linguistic tenacity, self-identity, and retention of cultural values have created the American mosaic in which colorful, individual pieces are fitted together to describe the lives of Americans.

Mosaic America

The American mosaic portrays the history of the nation and the diversity of its people. "Americans are a bundle of paradoxes; we are mixed in our origins, yet we are one people;"[2] a society that is dynamic, changing in every period of American history. America, a cultural mosaic of mankind, has the world at its doorstep. People of diverse cultural backgrounds continue to transform the face of urban America. Thirty-one cities increased in their ethnic populations within a decade.

"Someday soon... white America will become a minority. In the twenty-first century—and that's not far off—racial and ethnic groups in the United States will outnumber whites for the first time."[3] The "browning of America will alter everything in society, from politics and education to industry, values, and culture."[4] A number of ethnic organizations—such as Scotch, Irish, Italian, Polish, Hispanic, German, Asian, and Arabic—exist across the nation, whether for social, linguistic, professional, cultural, or artistic events. These organizations are already beginning to impact the infrastructure of the nation. Prior generations of immigrants quickly learned American English to survive and sought to "melt." The new immigrant is inseparable from the use of his language and cultural identity.

Institutions of higher education will be faced as to whether or not the core humanities curriculum will expand to reflect the cultures of Africa, Asia, Latin America, and other parts of the world. Books currently considered classics will be seen as cultural imperialism. History books will be prepared to reflect more than one view. There will be clashes over myths and icons in education. "Today's immigrants may be too much of a stretch for a nation based on western values."[5] America's ethnicity (see chart A) provides a view of the nation's ethnicity.

Oliver Wendell Holmes stated, "I find the great thing in the world is not so much where we stand as in what direction we are moving." The complexity of our society in the American global village requires that we expand our vision and creatively seek to understand that all people, especially ethnic/language-culture people, live in changing cultural patterns.

"Jesus Christ clothed the Father's love in human life to man. He was born in terms of natural limitation. Jesus acquired the

AMERICA'S ETHNICITY

Ethnic Group	1990	2000
Asian	4,063,894	4,663,167
Caribbean	805,709	924,522
European*	51,112,484	58,649,696
Hispanic (Including Puerto Rico)	23,254,836	28,761,893
North African & Middle Eastern	1,301,550	1,493,481
Native American	2,848,087	3,268,076
Pacific Islander	304,305	349,179
Sub-Sahara African	386,151	443,094
Totals	84,077,016	98,553,108
U.S.	253,024,479	271,493,439
% of U.S. Population Ethnic/Language Culture	33.2%	36.3%

*Excludes English, Welsh, Scottish, Irish and Multiple Ancestry.

Source: U.S. Census Publications: PC 80-S1-10; PC 80-S1-12; PC 80-1-B1; PC 80-1-C53A; P-25, No. 952 and P-25, No. 995. 2000 projections Language Church Extension, Home Mission Board.

cultural values, learned the language and accepted the rules and patterns of life that were a part of the social structure."[6]

Paul, the missionary, recognized culture as an invaluable vehicle for the communication process. A Roman citizen, he chose to be a Jew among Jews and a Greek among Greeks (1 Cor. 9:19-22). His missionary journeys took Paul to the urban areas of the known world. People of diverse cultures who spoke a variety of languages comprised the audiences among whom he sought to communicate the gospel.

Communication is a prime dynamic that determines the kind and rate of change in a society.[7] It involves relationships, an exchange of energy, challenges the individual beyond the status quo, and provides new insights and new attitudes toward people. "Communication is an agent of change that alters relationships between the minority group and the majority group. In a sense, each person/group adapts or relinquishes some of its tradition in an effort to exchange ideas and/or concepts, as in the case of religion, the concept of God."[8]

"Our myopic telling of history often causes us to ignore the sophistication of the many ethnic societies"[9] that comprise our nation, especially in the urban areas. This myopia causes us to stereotype people and assume that, because a person speaks "American English," he/she has been born and educated in the United States and is our friend, he/she has assimilated— "become just like us." In reality, ours is a mosaic nation that communicates in 636 languages and dialects and is composed of more than 500 ethnic groups. The myth of the melting-pot theory has proven that Americans, although encouraged and often forced to assimilate, continue to retain their visible identities, as well as their cultural heritages. The multicultural concept has been acknowledged by most Americans; yet there are those whose myopia continues to affect their perception of the American mosaic. The multicultural concept permits people to live in various phases of the chromatic scale of assimilation, thus becoming multilingual and multicultural, yet retaining their cultural identity and expression as a part of their life.

Christianity, in its effort to minister, has traditionally sought the isolated, the refugee, the immigrant, those whose language and culture are different from ours or those who have sought to be "like us." The immigrant church, whether from Europe, Latin America, Asia, or the South, has sought "its own kind" of people, becoming more of a "cultural club" than a New Testament church.

Historical and traditional lessons are to be learned from the immigrant church. The European church, for example, sought to minister among immigrants—"their own kind." The children began to acquire a knowledge of American English and some of the American cultural values. These European Americans gradually became invisible ethnics. The European church insisted on the use of their language and worship style and continually sought to minister to the new immigrant—the Nuclear Ethnic. Thus they gradually encouraged the European Americans, and later the generation of American Europeans, to go elsewhere to church. The American Europeans sought to become a part of the American/Anglo church, only to find that they were welcomed, but not accepted.

American ethnics are very much aware of the differences that exist. Frank Luna, Jr., of Dallas, was recently quoted by *U.S. News and World Report* as saying, "The prejudice is still there, but not like it used to be." The disenchantment with the church has seen the ethnic American and the American ethnic leave the church.

Regardless of how we feel, people are aware that in reality we are not all alike, and that some are more equal than others. Our cultural myopia needs to be replaced with a vision of the groups of "individuals who perceive themselves to have a common affinity for one another;"[10] "an affinity based upon language and culture"[11] and who cherish their heritage.

Unseen Americans

The American scene is, in a sense, unique in that there are the visible and the invisible ethnics. Yet within the invisible are those people who are not identified, since they comprise less than 1 percent of the population in a census tract. *The World Christian Encyclopedia* indicates that 500 ethnic groups have been identified in the United States. Ethnic groups come into being through the process of mobility. These unseen ethnics are in our midst; yet to our knowledge, the gospel has not been shared with these persons in our nation:

Fijians, Melanesian, Albanian, Basque, Moldavian, Dravidian, Nepalese, Bengalese, Aztec, Mayan, Zapotec, Aymara, Quechua, Trukese, Yapese, Maori, Tahitian, Tongan, Gypsies, Maltese, Turks, et cetera.

Immigrant America

The Immigration Act of 1965, established in memory of John F. Kennedy, abandoned the quota system that overwhelmingly favored the European character of the nation. This act of Congress invited the largest immigration since the early part of the century. These newcomers came and continue to come not from the Old World, but from the Third World. "All sides agree on one thing; immigration could be the most important outside force shaping the future of the U. S. through the next century."[12] No other country in the world has permitted its demographic mix to change so quickly, while believing that in so doing, it will be enriched by it. "Someday soon, . . . white Americans will become a minority group."[13] (See chart B.)

The Pacific Rim nations, often referred to as the Pacific challenge, "are multifaceted: economic, political strategic, even philosophical,"[14] as well as religious. The Pacific region has become the place where civilization is stepping up its pace. The ethnicity of the Pacific Rim nations is beyond our imagination. According to the *World Christian Encyclopedia,* there are in excess of 280 ethnic groups that use over 100 languages

U.S. POPULATION INCREASE
1980-1990

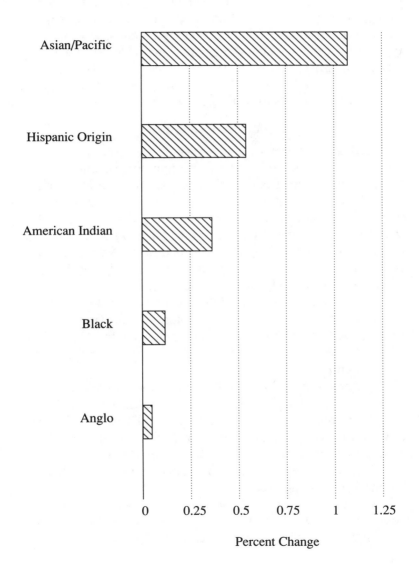

Percent Change

and more than 2,000 dialects. America's Pacific coastline is a twentieth century Asia Minor with a diversity of mores and languages. Most of these new Americans have found success and prosperity in their new home. Asia has replaced Europe as the leading source of United States engineers, doctors, and technical workers. Asian Americans own 400 Silicon Valley electronic firms, which in 1989 earned 2.5 billion dollars. Asians comprise 10 percent of California's population but 12.2 percent of the state's university enrollment.

Undocumented America

Americans have become increasingly alarmed by the number of undocumented people entering the country. These people come from Poland, Ethiopia, China, the Philippines, Latin America, Central America, and numerous other countries. Recently the Border Patrol encountered a group of Polish men who had traveled by airplane to Mexico and were being led by a "Coyote" across the Arizona desert. (Note: A Coyote is a person who leads individuals across the border illegally). Efforts are continually being made to enforce this country's existing laws on illegal entry. Surveys are conducted. Tempers flare. Economic sanctions are threatened. Yet without those undocumented people who reside in the United States and who provide the "stoop" labor, the cost of living in the nation would increase.

The immigrants (documented and undocumented) of the 1980s and 1990s are drawn, not from Europe, but overwhelmingly from the developing nations of the Third World, especially from Asia and Latin America. (See chart C.) 'These immigrants come in luxurious jetliners; not just as laborers, but as polished professionals, entrepreneurs, and refugees shaping the fabric of American society.

The decade of the 1980s brought nine million foreign-born people to the United States. In the 90s, five million children of immigrants are in the public schools. Three-and-a-half mil-

POPULATION INCREASE
NATURAL INCREASE & IMMIGRATION

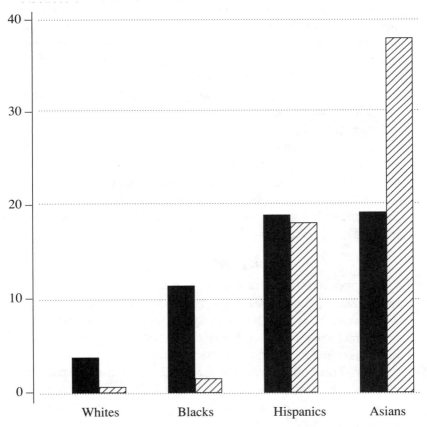

Annual rate per 1,000 population

Natural Increase (births minus deaths)   Net Immigration

lion of these children come from homes where English is not the first language. "More than 150 languages are represented in schools nationwide."[15] Seventy-three percent are of Hispanic heritage. Houston's Hearne Elementary School has 970 students who speak twenty-three languages in addition to American English. In Public School 217 in New York City, 40 percent of the children are immigrants who speak twenty-six languages, from Armenian to Urdu. On February 10, 1991, NBC News stated that there are 4.5 million elementary school children in the United States who speak 165 languages. Sixty-five percent speak Spanish.

"A new chapter in the history of immigrant America is about to begin."[16] Immigrants and refugees continue to come, giving new life and energy to communities and infusing new blood into the labor markets and economy; thereby, adding a diversity of sounds, sights, and life-styles to the urban areas. The "newcomers" will reinforce the validity of America and the richness of its culture and linguistic dimensions.

Demographic America

The population of the United States grew more slowly in the decade of the 1980s than in any decade since the Great Depression; however, the minority population grew sharply—thus forecasting social and political change that could define the twenty-first century. (See chart D.)

In 1990 one out of every four Americans defined himself as Hispanic or nonwhite. Current trends call for a 21 percent increase in the Hispanic population. By 2020 the number of residents will double to nearly 115 million. Asian presence will increase by 22 percent, blacks almost 12 percent; whites will probably decrease by 2 percent. By 2056, the average American will trace his or her heritage to Africa, Asia, the Hispanic world, the Pacific Islands, Arabia, or almost anywhere except white Europe. "The former majority will learn, as a normal

ETHNIC AMERICA

Ethnic Group	1990 Population	Percent Increase 1980-1990
ASIAN		
Chinese	1,645,472	104
Filipino	1,406,770	82
Japanese	847,562	21
Indian	815,447	126
Korean	798,849	125
Vietnamese	614,547	135
Laotian	149,014	213
Cambodian	147,411	819
Thai	91,275	102
Hmong	90,082	1,631
Pakistani	81,371	415
Indonesian	29,252	204
Malayan	12,243	200
Bangladeshi	11,838	801
Sri Lankan	10,970	275
Burmese	6,177	124
Okinawan	2,247	59
AMERICAN INDIANS, ESKIMOS, ALEUTS		
American Indian	878,285	38
Eskimo	57,152	36
Aleut	23,797	68
PACIFIC ISLANDERS		
Hawaiian	211,014	27
Samoan	62,964	50
Guamanian	49,345	53
Tongan	17,606	183
Fijian	7,036	148
Palauan	1,439	108
No. Mariana Islander	960	38
Tahitian	944	19
HISPANICS		
Mexican	13,495,938	54
Puerto Rican	2,727,754	35
Cuban	1,043,932	30
Other Hispanic	5,086,435	67

Source: U.S. Census Bureau, 1990 Census, Unpublished report.

part of everyday life, the meaning of the Latin slogan engraved on the U.S. coins—*e pluribus unum*—one formed from many.

Linguistic America

Languages are a product of cultural evolution. Linguistic paleoanthropologists are reconstructing the origin of the world's 5,000 languages. "Language is an integral part of the cultural glue that binds people together and signals their presence."[17] The United States, ethnically the most heterogenous nation in the world, is the most linguistically homogenous. Yet *The World Christian Encyclopedia* lists English as one of twenty-six major languages spoken by Americans. In addition, there are more than 600 other languages and dialects, or 636 languages and dialects used by Americans daily.

In reality, Americans do not speak English. The American English spoken reflects the history, the development, and the continuing immigration or globalization of the nation. American English has a vocabulary of words, 51 percent of which are German in origin and include words of Arabic, Latin, Spanish, and Greek origin. "All living languages are constantly changing."[18] Thus just as the languages immigrating to America are influenced by American English, so is American English being influenced and undergoing constant change. The immigrant languages that displaced the indigenous languages have emerged in the twentieth century as American English.

Religious America

The recent survey commissioned by the City University of New York Graduate School provides a view into the religious affiliation of Americans. The study of fifty denominations, including Taoist and Hindu, cuts across racial, ethnic, class, regional, and generational lines. The response indicates that for many Americans, religious identity is important. Among the findings are these:

1. Hispanics make up 14 percent of all Catholics.
2. Sixty-five percent of the Hispanics are Catholics.
3. Most Irish are Protestant.
4. Half of black U.S. residents are Baptists; nine percent are Catholic.
5. Pentecostals have the lowest median age—39.8.
6. Presbyterians have the highest median age—48.2.
7. Baptists' median age is 44.1.
8. Jewish are most urban with 96 percent, followed by Catholic, 84.5 percent; Episcopalian, 83.5 percent; Presbyterian, 77.8 percent; Mormon, 72.9 percent; Lutheran, 71.2 percent; Pentecostal, 69 percent; Methodist, 66.3 percent; and Baptist, 66.1 percent.

The survey does not gauge the people's commitment, only their religious identity.

Buying of America

"Foreign money is changing the face of America, the lives of Americans, and the nature of our political processes."[19] The surge of foreign investments is rebuilding the cities, reshaping rural America, and providing jobs for millions of Americans. Foreign investors have discovered a haven on our shores, enriching our lives by introducing new cultures, languages, and religions. Pragmatic Americans do not care where the money comes from as long as jobs are provided and economic growth stimulated. Private investors are being replaced by foreign investors as the major purchasers of U.S. government securities. "Foreigners are our bankers. The era of the American economic independence is gone, thanks to a trade deficit too big to fund ourselves. Foreigners increasingly influence inflation and recession in the United States."[20]

Representatives of several state governments regularly greet each other on the streets of Hong Kong and Brussels as they seek foreign investors to create jobs in their respective states.

These investors often request the easing of the tax climate, tax concessions, improvements to infrastructures, and special services. In 1981 foreign investments of $180 billion provided more than three million Americans with employment.

Foreign investments bring a significant number of people from their respective nations to operate the new industries, et cetera. These people, in turn, bring their languages, cultures, and religious beliefs to America. In a sense, the global mission field is coming to America. The church has the opportunity to proclaim the gospel globally by evangelizing and planting churches among these internationals who reside in America for a short period of time. The church today and into the next century must learn to present the biblical message in the ethnolinguistic context of the internationals. Foreign investments can reshape the nation into a materialistic society. However, the church must aggressively seek to evangelize the investor, proclaim the gospel globally, and plant churches around the world.

A Diverse Megapolis

Eleven families from the town of Alamos, Sonora, Mexico, established Los Angeles as an agricultural settlement in 1781. By 1860 the population included Chinese immigrants, Basque sheepherders, peasants from France and Germany, and German-Jewish merchants.

Today people from 140 countries are represented among the 8.5 million residents. Los Angeles is the second largest Mexican, Armenian, Korean, Filipino, and Salvadorian city in the world. There are more Canadians in Los Angeles than in Vancouver, British Columbia. Los Angeles has more Samoans than American Samoa.

Eighty-three percent of the 600,000 public school children in Los Angeles identify with an ethnic group. These children speak ninety-six languages and represent seventy-seven ethnic groups. Thirty adult schools teach English as a second language to over 200,000 people. They have a waiting list of about 50,000 people. The universities have enrolled more than twelve thousand foreign students from more than one hundred seventy-five countries.

"Los Angeles is the nucleus of American business for the Pacific Rim nations."[21] Foreign investment in real estate staggers the imagination. Los Angeles is the capital of Korean business in the nation. A Filipino immigrant, who came in 1972, today owns an auto dealership that makes sales in fifty different languages. The increase of foreign investments has attracted more than 70,000 professionals. Korean cultural traits, such as bowing, are practiced by the California Bank in Koreatown.

The ethnic groups are beginning to exercise political power. Their influence is noted by the bilingual street signs, the diversity of the police force, and the makeup of the various political entities.

The three million Hispanics in Los Angeles County grew by 22 percent in a five-year period and will outnumber the Anglos by 2010. The Hispanic community is composed, on various socioeconomic and educational levels, of illiterates to millionaire professionals.

Southern California includes people from twenty Asian cultures. Asian immigrants began to arrive in substantial number in the mid 1970s. They struggled to succeed; however, their children have established roots and are seeking to become middle-class Americans. In 1987 Asians received nearly half all college degrees.

Western Europeans arrived in Los Angeles in the mid-nineteenth century, that is, Scots, Germans, French, Baltics, Dutch, Greeks, Gypsies, Irish, Italians, Polish, Russians, Scandinavians, and Yugoslavs. Eastern Europeans, primarily Russians, have immigrated in the twentieth century.

Middle Eastern political boundaries are not often easy to determine. Today, in Los Angeles, there are 300,000 Arabs,

250,000 Armenians, 350,000 Iranians, 200,000 Israelis, 50,000 Palestinians, and those from Yemen and other small nations. East Hollywood is known as "Little Armenia." Most of the Arabs are well-educated professionals. They have come because of the climate, economic opportunity, and ethnic diversity.

The 1980 Census reported over 16,000 people in Los Angeles from African nations, such as Nigeria, Ethiopia, Cape Verde Islands, Ghana, and other sub-Saharan nations. The Ethiopian population exceeds 20,000 and the Kenyan over 1,000. The people from these nations celebrate their traditional festivals and are becoming a viable community.

Invisible immigrants from Australia, New Zealand, South Africa, and Canada look and act so much like Americans that they are overlooked. These are primarily professional people.

American migrants, Native Americans and American blacks, are constantly adding to the population of Los Angeles. It is estimated that there are more than 200,000 American Indians, making Los Angeles' Indian population larger than the Navajo Reservation. African-Americans exceed a million in population and are a vibrant group.

Twenty-first century Los Angeles will "be home to more races, religions, cultures, languages, and people than any other city in the world."[22] It will increasingly become a multiracial and multicultural city. The intermarriage of races and cultures will give birth to the twenty-first century American.

Bicultural and bilingual persons will combine these with the American experience to become tricultural and trilingual. They will, in all probability, be comfortable in any of the three languages and cultures, be selective, or develop an entirely new culture and American dialect. Organizations such as the church will be faced with the challenge to meet the needs of the twenty-first century American.

Missions in America

James Sullivan in his book, *Baptist Polity as I See It,* states that, "The work of the Home Mission Board is getting more complex all the time because of an ever-enlarging influx of many and vast ethnic groups who still speak their native tongues."[23] These groups add new cultural dimensions to the American way of life. Sullivan adds, "The work of the Home Mission Board is getting more complex all the time because of an ever-enlarging influx of many and vast ethnic groups who still speak their native tongues."[24] In some ways, it becomes more complex as leaders must not only seek to penetrate the ethnic mission field, but also seek to update the historical and traditional infrastructures of the denomination.

The traditional leader—pastor, missionary, missions director (associational, state and/or agency)—must be compassionately motivated and seek to become a missions statesman. This statesman's leadership should be based upon sound principles. He should be able to handle delicate matters, be influential, wise, versed in intercultural relationships, capable of making decisions, appreciated by his/her peers, and willing to accept responsibility.

Measuring the impact on the mission field is more than statistics. According to Sullivan, "All agencies must keep in mind constantly that while good business and organizational procedures are to be understood and respected, that Southern Baptists do not exist for the purpose of carrying on efficient business enterprises."[25] The spiritual always takes priority. Sullivan adds that "Religious leaders must have the highest regard and even love for the people with whom they work daily."[26]

Be a friend; understand what is meant, not said; know, appreciate, and respect the heritage and culture of each person and/or congregation. Seek to speak in their behalf—not for them. Help them to understand the American way of life, but don't mold them into a model of oneself. "Leadership

[must] be manifested because in spiritual realms no person can be driven."[27]

The successful leader is the statesman who seeks to change the world. Leaders are people with "a goal, a vision, a cause, and a commitment."[28] Those who succeed are "highly intelligent, highly disciplined, hard workers, self-confident, and driven by a dream"[29] and able to "look beyond the horizon."

Leaders should have the ability to relate within their own culture, as well as among diverse cultures. These people will need to feel secure in their own identities, while accommodating to the language and culture of others. These leaders are best characterized as being flexible, risk oriented, creative and ambitious, and capable of being understood in two or more senses. They utilize their heritage(s), culture(s), and language(s) in their efforts to minister and witness in a diverse ethnolinguistic setting.

The following is an attempt to describe the types of leaders who, hopefully, would be capable of taking the variable components of management and intercultural relationships and synchronizing these with statistics to achieve contextual church growth:

1. **CE—Culturally Exposed**—a person who is aware of the uniqueness of other cultures, flexible in relating to others, and whose attitude leads to a desire to become knowledgeable.

2. **CS—Culturally Sensitive**—a person who is aware of cultural variances, appreciates other cultures, and who permits others to function within their cultural context.

3. **CA—Culturally Adaptable**—a person who is secure in his/her culture and who seeks to adapt to other cultures when relating to other people.

4. **LC—Language Cultural**—a person who seeks to become compatible in a language and culture in addition to his/her own.

5. **EL—Ethnolinguistic**—a person whose heritage and language is other than Anglo.
6. **MC—Multicultural**—a person capable of living, working, thinking, et cetera, in a multicultural environment simultaneously.
7. **NL—Natural Leader**—a person who emerges as a leader from among the people and who preferably is bilingual and bicultural.

Sharing the gospel in a pluralistic society in essence calls for the development of the contextualized/denominational/indigenous church. It should be contextualized in that the gospel is woven into the culture of the group and gradually influences the value system in keeping with biblical teachings. It should be denominational in that it becomes an active part of, is accepted by, and contributes to the life of the denomination. In a sense, it nourishes as well as receives nourishment from its relationships, one with each other. It should be indigenous in that it supports itself in keeping with the ability of the particular group and uses its natural, social, and cultural channels for multiplying the body of Christ.

The "Ten Forces Reshaping America," according to the March 19, 1984 issue of *U.S. News and World Report,* include two forces that are pertinent to our task. These are foreign competition and the rise of minorities, both of which are related to the urban scene.

Foreign competition is leading American firms to manufacture products overseas. The attitude that "if you can't beat them, join them"[30] will result in greater unemployment, as well as foreign investment in the United States; both of which will impact the majority of language-culture people.

The minorities, "once treated as second class citizens, are putting their imprint on every aspect of American life."[31] The 1950s and 1960s, combined with new patterns of immigration, lessened the domination by the white value system and have "evolved an America with far more diversity."[32] Immigration from Asia and Latin America means an increasing number of ethnics entering the urban areas. The American ethnics are assuming leadership roles and are seeking "a fair share of the wealth and influence."[33]

"The indelible marks of change are everywhere; and the seeds for future twists and turns are sprouting."[34] Like it or not, change will be swifter in the future, predicts Marvin Cetron, president of Forecasting International, primarily in the metropolitan areas of the nation.

The ethnic diversity of the nation, especially in the urban areas, challenges the church as the twenty-first century dawns. The increasing activity of Muslims, Buddhists, Hindus, and adherents of numerous other religions should make Christians realize the urgency of evangelizing America, especially the urban areas. "The mission movement of the New Testament was primarily an urban movement."[35] The urban settings are the final arena for missions.

Notes

1. "Remapping American Culture," *U.S. News and World Report* (Washington, D.C.: U.S. News and World Report, Inc., December 4, 1989), 60.

2. David Hackett Fischer, *Albion's Seed* (New York: Oxford University Press, 1989), 3.

3. "Remapping American Culture," *U.S. News and World Report* (Washington, D.C." U.S. News and World Report, Inc., Dec. 4, 1989), 28.

4. *U.S. News and World Report,* 28.

5. *U.S. News and World Report,* 31.

6. Oscar I. Romo, "Ethnic Missions in America" (Atlanta: Home Mission Board, unpublished paper, 1978), 22.

7. R. Daniel Shaw, *Transculturation* (Pasadena: William Carey Library, 1988), 19.

8. David J. Hasselgrave and Edward Rommen, *Contextualization* (Grand Rapids: Baker Book House, 1988), 1.

9. James N. Lewis Jr., "American Pluralism" (Atlanta: Home Mission Board, unpublished paper, 1980), 3.

10. Edward R. Dayton and David A. Fraser, *Planning Strategies for World Evangelization* (Grand Rapids, Michigan: William B. Eerdmans Publishing Co., 1980), 37.

11. Dayton and Fraser, 37.

12. *The Christian Science Monitor* (Boston: The Christian Science Publishing Society, January 2, 1990).

13. "America's Changing Colors," *Time* (New York: *Time* magazine, April 9, 1990), 28.

14. David Aikman, *Pacific Rim* (Boston: Little Brown and Co., 1986), 4.

15. *Newsweek* (New York: Newsweek, Inc., February 11, 1991), 57.

16. Alejandro Portes and Ruben G. Rumbaut, *Immigrant America* (Berkeley: University of California, 1990), vii.

17. *U.S. News and World Report* (Washington, D.C.: U.S. News and World Report, Inc., November 5, 1990), 60.

18. Eugene A. Nida, *Customs and Cultures* (South Pasadena: William Carey Library, 1975), 208.

19. Martin and Susan Tolchin, *Buying into America* (New York: Time Books, 1988), 3.

20. Tolchin, 11.

21. Zena Pearlstone, *Ethnic Los Angeles,* (Beverly Hills, Calif.: Hillcrest Press, 1990), 39.

22. Pearlstone, 135.

23. James L. Sullivan, *Baptist Polity as I See It* (Nashville: Broadman Press, 1983), 128.

24. Ibid., 128.

25. Ibid., 128.

26. Ibid., 216.

27. Ibid., 223.

28. Ibid.

29. Richard Nixon, *Leaders* (New York: Warner Brothers, Inc., 1982), 3.

30. *U.S. News and World Report,* 49-53.

31. Ibid.

32. Ibid.

33. Ibid.

34. Ibid.

35. Roger Greenway and Timothy M. Monsma, *Cities, Missions' New Frontiers* (Grand Rapids: Baker Book House, 1989), 13.

3 The Gospel in a Pluralistic Context

"The Christian movement exists in a world that is characterized by changes. People are affected by these changes. Their spiritual needs do not change with the passing of time, but these may be expressed in different ways."[1]

Historically, America is composed of people with diverse linguistic and cultural heritages. These people, whether American Indian, European, Hispanic, Arabic, or Asian, are immigrants or the children of immigrants. Although efforts have been made to melt these groups, their desire to be who they are has led them to identify themselves with a language-culture group.

America's true character is "that we are a common culture which is composed of diverse cultures."[2] The acceptance of the multiculutral concept is acknowledged by most Americans. This concept permits people to live in various phases of their linguistic and cultural heritage simultaneously, thus becoming multilingual and multicultural. Yet they are capable of retaining their unique cultural and linguistic life-styles.

Ethnicity in the Early Church

Language and culture have been the vehicles through which God has communicated His redeeming love through the ages. The linguistic diversity of the ancient world appears in biblical stories such as the Tower of Babel and the Day of Pentecost.

"By counting the people enumerated in Genesis 10, the rabbis later figured at 72 the number (of languages) spoken in the Ancient World."[3]

Jesus Christ clothed the Father's love in human life to man. He was born in terms of natural limitations. Jesus acquired the cultural values, learned the language, and accepted rules and patterns of life that were a part of the social structure.

Jesus was a missionary, sent by the Father to redeem the *ta ethne.*

Paul, the missionary, recognized language and culture as invaluable vehicles for the communication process. A Roman citizen, he adapted culturally and linguistically whether among Jews or Greeks (1 Cor. 9:19-22). To the best of my knowledge, at no time did he ask the "hearer" to become like him, but began with those circumstances that related to the people (Acts 17:22-23).

The Galatian church was a cultural (Celtic) congregation. The people were simple, open-hearted, curious, and gullible. Paul found them hospitable.

The Corinthian church was a cultural group who insisted that the Gentile Christians should follow the Mosaic law. The Corinthians were pushy, argumentative, and conceited.

The Thessalonians, Philippians, and Romans were each distinctive in temperament, culture, custom, and attitude. Although the early churches were bound by a definite unity of a personal experience with Jesus Christ, it was not uniformity.

Language and culture were the vehicles through which the biblical message of salvation was communicated.

The Church in a Pluralistic Society

A theology of pluralism for today calls for an understanding of the nature and function of the church. Christ came into a world similar to ours. He taught the truth about God, man, righteousness, and evil. Having revealed the truth, Christ reconciled evil men to God. He dispelled fear and gave hope to the hopeless. He placed infinite value on human life. Jesus commissioned those to whom He gave life, the church, to share this life and truth with others.

God's love is received by receiving His Son as personal Savior and Lord. Church members can reshape their destiny and the congregation to which they belong by understanding and applying John's meaning, "But as many as received him, to them gave he power to become the sons of God. . . . Which were born, not of blood, nor of the will of man, but of God" (John 1:12-13).

The church is divine in its origin and not merely a human institution.[4] The word *church* with its cognate form *kirk*, is derived from the Greek word *kyriakon*, signifying "the Lord's" or "belonging to the Lord."[5] The New Testament equivalent *ecclesia* was originally employed to denote an assembly or congregation of free citizens summoned or "called out" in connection with public affairs.[6] It often refers to the occasion when a specific congregation gathers for prayer, instruction, and/or deliberation.

The concept of the church, which is basic in Christian history, has a wide difference in particular Christian bodies with regards to the nature of the teachings of the New Testament. In this, as in many other matters, Baptists are distinct. The church is autonomous in its operation and has the responsibility to proclaim the gospel. The Book of Acts describes the church as an assembly of believers who prayed and were led by the Holy Spirit, united in fellowship, missionary in outreach, and contributed of its possessions. Beginning in the community of Jerusalem, the church seeks to share the gospel with all people, regardless of their ethnic uniqueness. The local church, in cooperation with other local churches, unites its efforts and resources to share the gospel in accordance with the mandate of Jesus Christ.[7]

The church owes its existence to God. It is His creation through Jesus Christ. The nature of the church can best be understood when its members understand who they are, what they are to do, and how they are to do it.

A church is a congregation of the children of God. Consider the significance of the word: "Behold, what manner of love the Father hath bestowed upon us, that we should be called the sons of God" (1 John 3:1). A person becomes a child of God as a result of God's love in action. The love bestowed upon us should not be taken lightly, for "while we were yet sinners, Christ died for us" (Rom. 5:8).

Being a child of God is a growing relationship. Each child is given the power to become a living, growing, new creation. Christian growth is essential on the part of the children of God. As children, we are called to reflect His nature to the world. As Christ revealed the purpose of His coming, so should church members reveal the purpose for which God called them: to be His children. To succeed, each person and congregation must continually give attention to maintaining their relationship with God. Church members are not only the children of God; they are also brothers in Christ. "In Christ" means to live in the reconciling love of God, a love that cannot be understood in human terms alone. One must understand something of the love of God. "Herein is love, not that we loved God, but that He loved us, and sent His son to be the propitiation for our sins. Beloved, if God so loved us, we ought to love one another" (1 John 4:10-11).

The fellowship of love among believers should be the most outstanding characteristic among the congregation. The fellowship is held together by Christ, for He is the common bond by which the fellowship is first created. Christ is the common bond by which the fellowship understands its purpose and receives its power. When Christ dwells in the lives of church members, a unity of heart, mind, and purpose result; when Christ lives through the lives of church members, a fellowship beyond mere human experience develops. They are drawn together through His Spirit to live His life. The church is the body of Christ. Paul wrote, "Now ye are the body of Christ, and members in particular" (1 Cor. 12:27). God sent Jesus to carry out a mission that had been planned since the foundation of the world. Jesus established the church that it might continue this mission.

The church is a community of believers who have been gathered from the inhabitants of a specific area or group. To be sure, it meets in assembly; but it is constituted as *ecclesia* prior to and apart from such assembly. The area from which it is gathered may be a single household (Rom. 16:5; Col. 4:15; Philem. 2), a single city, such as Jerusalem (Acts 8:1; 11:22), Cenchrea (Rom. 16:1), Corinth (1 Cor. 1:2; 2 Cor. 1:1), Thessalonica (1 Thess. 1:1; 2 Thess. 1:1), Ephesus (Rev. 2:1), or a province such as Galatia (Gal. 1:2), Judea (Gal. 1:22; 1 Thess. 2:14), Macedonia (2 Cor. 8:1), or Asia (1 Cor. 16:19; Rev. 1:4, 11). Many congregations in a specific area may be represented by the noun in plural, as well as the singular (Acts 9:31). A group of congregations may be designated by reference to a common racial and cultural origin (e.g., the churches of the Gentiles, Rom. 16:4). In all of the above, the basic function is to identify, without qualifying adjectives, a particular congregation or group of congregations. The idea of "having been gathered" persists in virtually all these contexts.

The nature of the communities, therefore, is continually qualified by the One who summons or gathers it (Acts. 20:23; 1 Cor. 1:2; 10:32; 11:16, 22; 15:9; 2 Cor. 1:1; Gal. 1:13; 1 Thess. 2:14; 2 Thess. 1:4; 1 Tim 3:5, 15). The *ecclesia* belongs to God because He called it into being, dwells within it, rules over it, and accomplishes His purpose through it. Whether singular or plural, the community is considered a single unit. It has been gathered by the one God. A worldwide community is embodied in a localized form where a congregation exists.

The church is a living body. Every living body must grow. Its development is the clearest evidence that it is alive. From the

Day of Pentecost, the church manifested the vital force given by the Holy Spirit. The apostles were to preach the gospel "in Jerusalem, and in all Judea, and in Samaria, and unto the uttermost part of the earth" (Acts 1:8). The church is commissioned to evangelize (Matt. 28:19-20). Thus the church provides the channel through which the message of salvation is communicated to *ta ethne.*

This mission makes possible for all people, regardless of cultural heritage, linguistic abilities, economic, or social status, to be capable of becoming a child of God. Just as a physical body has many parts, so a congregation is a body with many parts. Not all have the same function, but they do have a single purpose. Christ is the head of the church, giving direction to the whole body. The church in a pluralistic society is composed of people who, in addition to spiritual gifts, may also have gifts of a cultural heritage and the ability to communicate in a language(s) other than the one used by the dominant group. Although the church is not called to reflect the ethnic composition of the community, the unique characteristics of its members make possible the carrying out of the great command: Go ye (or as you go); therefore, make disciples of *ta ethne.*

The church as a body should encourage its members to use their cultural and linguistic gifts. The use of these gifts should not produce pride or envy nor cause dissension in the church. These gifts may be used by individuals or groups within the church to minister to the needs of others. The user of these gifts should always keep in mind Paul's statement to the Romans, "For as we have many members in one body, and all members have not the same offices: So we, being many, are one body in Christ, and every one members one of another" (Rom. 12:4-5). The church, the body of Christ, may be composed of people of diverse cultures, languages, and life circumstances that make possible the opportunity for each individual to use his gift(s) to share God's message, to serve, to teach, to encourage, to lead, and to share in accordance with God's grace. These gifts are used for the edification of the church.

When Paul speaks of Christian believers "all one in Christ," he is describing the reality that those in Christ, although they may have ethnic, linguistic, and cultural differences, were transcended by their "being-in-Christness." In Christ are many cultures that may reflect an experience with Jesus Christ. These cultures are components within the confines of a dominant way of life in a pluralistic society.

A new dimension of life, for the new believer, begins when the blueprint for behavioral patterns, cultural values, and linguistic usage, becomes imbued with the love of Christ. There seems to emerge a new sense of identity and worthiness. To become a "Christian" is not to negate one's culture and language, but to add new dimensions to the way of life.

Several years ago while visiting a Hispanic church in Las Vegas, the pastor asked me to accompany him to a Bible study meeting. The meeting was held in a restaurant of the casino where the only other participant, a dealer, worked. Neither the pastor nor the dealer had a Bible; yet they discussed various Scripture references. After several minutes of discussion, the dealer said, "Pastor, it seems to me that my new life in Christ calls for me to secure another type of employment. Please help me to acquire other skills so I can support my family." The man had not ceased to be a dealer nor a Hispanic to become a Christian. He was seeking to acquire another dimension to his life that permitted him to support his family because he had become "a new creature" in Christ.

A study of twenty Hispanic Southern Baptist churches was conducted in an effort to determine the effect of the gospel on ten selected cultural factors. The factors were pride, brujeria (witchcraft), family, fellowship, possessions, language, compadrazco (intimate, non-family relationship), education, time, and food. These were evaluated as to their strengths, with ten being the highest, before and after acquiring a new life-style—

conversion to Christianity. The results indicate the value of fellowship, language usage, possessions, education, and time increased. The value of food, family, and pride did not change. Only two declined; these were brujeria and compadrazco. (See chart on next page.)

At least three observations can be made concerning the study: (1) when a Hispanic has a conversion experience it does not mean that the cultural heritage is negated; (2) the cultural factors, regardless of their value, continue to influence the behavior of a person; and (3) the value of the cultural factors does change in keeping with the interpretation of Scripture.

Churches ministering in a pluralistic society should consider the principles of inclusiveness, freedom, and community from a pragmatic viewpoint. Inclusiveness implies an openness to all groups or individuals regardless of cultural or linguistic heritage. Freedom implies a type of liberty in which groups or individuals are free to create their own fashion, worship, and activities using the language in which they best communicate. Community implies a recognition that all men and groups have the right to exist and are interdependent. Paul's theology of call, "But as God hath distributed to every man, as the Lord hath called every one, so let him walk" (1 Cor. 7:17), can be understood as an assurance that to become a believer does not require the negation of one's cultural heritage. Paul taught that people need not cross cultural, linguistic, or class barriers to become Christians. One can best understand the significance of the gospel when it is shared within the context of one's life.

The United States in Perspective

America, now more than two hundred years old, faces the crises of a still emerging nationhood, with a puzzle of cultural diversities. The world is in constant change as mobility and technology increase. People from throughout the global village will come to our nation, either legally or illegally. These

CULTURAL FACTORS
U.S. Southern Baptist

Cultural-value strengths are rated on a scale of 1 to 10, with 10 as the strongest.

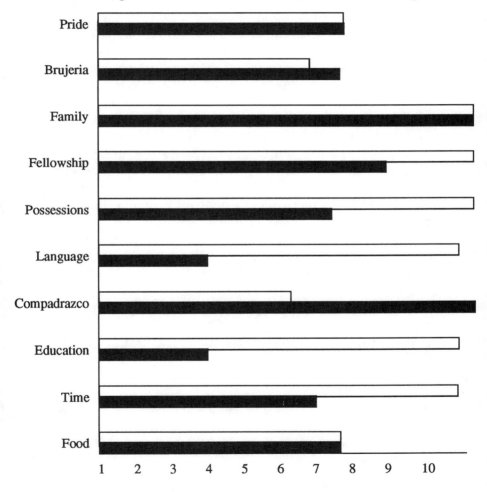

■ Prior to evangelical life-style

☐ Since acquiring evangelical life-style

people will bring with them languages and cultures currently unknown in our land. Severing their relations back home will provide opportunities for witness and ministry.

Pluralistic Society

America may be referred to as a twentieth-century Tower of Babel, a pluralistic society dispersed across an entire continent. It is an aggregate of peoples of different groups who have retained their own heritages, cultures, languages, and lifestyles. Ethnic groups perceive themselves as alike by virtue of common ancestry and are so regarded by others. More than 120 million Americans, excluding American blacks, consider themselves as belonging to one of 500 ethnic groups who communicate in one or more of 636 languages and dialects. This is in addition to the aliens (internationals), the six million illegals, and fourteen million deaf and hearing-impaired persons.

America's pluralism is that of an immigrant society that never acquired a territorial base. Different groups reside in different parts of the country; they did originally and continue to do so by choice, clustering for companionship, protection, and survival.[8] By choice they continue to retain their identities, cultural heritages, and linguistic abilities. Ethnic identification gives meaning to life, yet permits a strong and loyal support for the American way of life.[9]

American Diversity

The diversity of people who comprise the American pluralism calls for a broad overview of the sociological triangle. The triangle categorizes people as follows. (See triangle chart.)

1. **Nuclear Ethnic**—people who immigrated to or were born in the United States; yet they live in an isolated setting from the mainstream of American life.

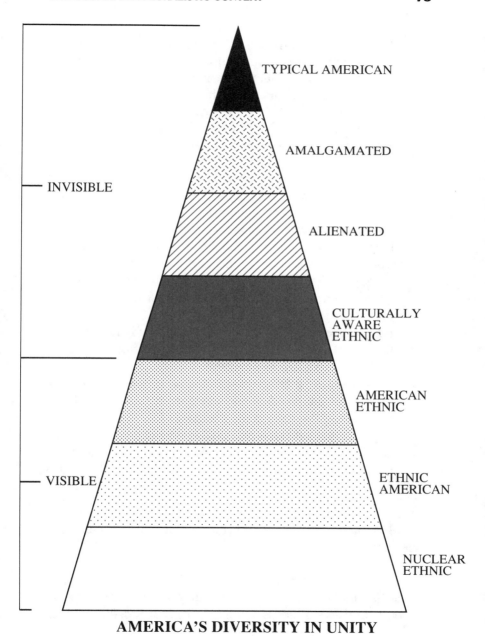

AMERICA'S DIVERSITY IN UNITY

2. **Ethnic American**—people who identify themselves with a language-culture group, immigrated to the United States and are American citizens. They often refer to their countries of origin as "home." Their identity contributes to their cultural heritages and tenacious usage of a language other than American English.

3. **American Ethnic**—people who identify with a language-culture group and who were born, raised, and educated in the United States. They are bilingual and bicultural and are capable of living in two worlds simultaneously; yet they are proud of their heritage.

4. **Culturally Aware Ethnic**—people who identify with a language-culture group when it is convenient and beneficial. In most cases, their knowledge of a language other than American English is limited. The invisible ethnic easily becomes lost among the masses. The visible ethnic often tries to lose himself.

5. **Alienated Ethnic**—people whose visibility identifies them; yet their relationships with their ethnic heritages and languages are nonexistent.

6. **Amalgamated Ethnic**—people who are constantly in search of their heritage and are uncomfortable in whichever setting they are at the moment.

7. **Typical American**—people whose "wide spectrum of culture reflects the fact that American culture is composed of diverse cultures," according to Michael Novak.[10]

Ours is a generation with the responsibility of sharing the gospel in the midst of changing cultural patterns in a pluralistic society.[11]

Channels for Proclamation

The Father's love for human life came to mankind through the birth and life of Jesus Christ. Jesus learned the cultural values, language(s) of the day, and accepted social structure's rules and patterns of life.

The Book of Acts indicates that Paul acknowledged culture as a valuable vehicle for communicating. Paul was a Roman citizen, yet he chose to be a Jew among the Jews and a Greek among the Greeks (1 Cor. 9:19-22).

Language and Culture

Language and culture are vital parts of a person's heritage; a heritage with diverse ethnic, racial, religious, and social aspects that may exist as autonomous components within the confines of a common way of life. Life in a pluralistic society is unique to the American heritage.

People are bound together by culture. Culture becomes the blueprint for living as well as governing the usage of the various languages. This blueprint prescribes behavior, beliefs, values, and skills.

The world's linguistic categories represent some five thousand speech communities which may number from less than a thousand to several million. Joy, love, hate, and knowledge are acquired and shared through the various language and cultural patterns. The cultural experience provides the basis for the development of values, premises, beliefs, opinions, and meaning of life.

Thus cultural life-style is living in accord with a person's background. This includes language, dress, food, value system, and other characteristics of the particular culture.

Ethnic Grouping

Ethnic groups have several basic characteristics that define their nature and distinguish them from other groups. Ethnic groups occupy distinct niches in the social and natural environment to which they adapt themselves. There are 500 types of ethnic groups in America. The following are the categories of ethnic groupings.

1. **Tribal—** occupy a single territory that is the "barrio," "across the tracks," or "poverty".
2. **Polyethnic**—these may occupy or share territory with other ethnic groups. These may gradually replace one another or become interdependent on each other.
3. **Caste systems**—these are people who belong to a common social system; primarily laborers who perform certain jobs which others do not want.
4. **Minorities**—there are dominant societies that reject ethnic groups who live apart from the rest of the people.

Members of minority groups are denied access to status positions; they are isolated and live within their own values. Their identities, imposed by society, usually provide little possibility for assimilation into the dominant population.

All people are born helpless; that is, without a culture, language, or the ability to survive alone. Yet within a short time, they are molded into a cultural or linguistic distinction. Enculturation begins at birth and continues throughout life.

Cultural Context

Context consists of those aspects of life that influence our existence, protection, relationships, and survival. The American context varies as to the region, location, and aspirations. It is a constantly changing context influenced by worldwide incidents. Regardless of our opportunities or circumstances, we tend to retreat to that context in which we are comfortable. For instance, it has been my privilege to travel, not only across the nation, but throughout the world. This has given me opportunities to associate with leaders of various governments, diplomats, and religious leaders of many nations, with the poor as well as the wealthy. This included having at my disposal chauffeur-driven limousines. Yet I am most comfortable in my own house, talking with my neighbor, and driving my own car.

The contextual factors are many; however, the following will help to communicate effectively:

1. **Regional culture**—denoted by the dialect spoken, type of food consumed, and relationships (that is, South, Texan, etc.)
2. **Cultural identity**—whether the person is a visible ethnic or an invisible ethnic (that is, Hungarian, Cuban, German, Hispanic, etc.)
3. **Language**—the vocal sounds, the pronunciation, the dialect, and the vocabulary; the person's acquaintance with the language.

Cultural Symbols

1. Greetings
   a. Americans shake hands.
   b. Asians bow.
   c. Hispanics embrace.
   d. Russians embrace and kiss.
2. Host
   a. Anglos say, "Come to see me"; in essence saying, "Set an appointment."
   b. Hispanics say, "My house is your house."
   c. Asians receive guests with humility.
3. Respect
   a. Asians usually respect their elders.
   b. Americans often respect the person of influence or "position."
4. Crossing the street
   a. Americans look to the left.
   b. Japanese look to the right.
5. Eating a piece of pie
   a. Americans turn the pie to point at them.
   b. British turn the wide crust of the pie toward them.
6. Dismiss
   a. Anglos say good-bye to a guest.
   b. Hispanics embrace the guest.

    c. Asians escort guests to their vehicles and wave as they depart.
7. Clothing
    a. Americans wear short sleeves in the summer.
    b. People from the Middle East are covered.
8. Food
    a. Americans eat cereal and eggs for breakfast.
    b. Mexicans eat a piece of sweet bread or a tortilla.
9. Eating utensils
    a. Americans eat with their right hands and use forks.
    b. Europeans eat with forks in their left hands.
    c. Asians use chopsticks.
    d. Arabs use their hands.
10. Automobiles
    a. Americans drive in the right lane.
    b. British drive in the left lane.

Language

The linguistic dimensions of the world are classified into 5,000 speech communities, which provide the basis for 5,106 spoken languages.[12] Some of these communities may number in the millions; others may have less than a thousand members. Through linguistic patterns people express their joy, love, and hate, as well as share and acquire knowledge. The dimensions of the patterns symbolize unity, understanding, and misunderstanding in the usage of terminology, type, meaning, significance, and accent. These patterns are based on values, premises, beliefs, opinions, and meaning of life in keeping with the acquired cultural experience.

The language not only denotes the linguistic family—Spanish, German, et cetera—but also the area of the world and country. The pronunciation indicates dialect, rapidity (that is, Cubans, Mexicans from Mexico, Anglos from Brooklyn, Southerners). The vocabulary provides an insight as to the person's education—illiterate or literate. The manner of expression will indicate if there is joy, sadness, deja vu.

Linguistic Changes

"Living languages are constantly changing."[13] The English of Chaucer's *Canterbury Tales* has undergone much change since the fourteenth century. Americans may recognize many of the words of the archaic character of contemporary English spelling; but if these words were recited by a person from the Middle East, it is doubtful we would recognize a single phrase. English is not alone in changing; all languages change. Languages undergo vocabulary changes as the cultural context changes and words are borrowed from the outside world. American English is basically a Germanic language. Yet thousands of words have been borrowed from other languages: *chant* and *village* from French; *spaghetti* and *bologna* from Italian; *patio* and *vamoose* from Spanish; *consul* and *senator* from Latin; *theolog* and *hippodrome* from Greek; *chocolate* and *tomato* from Aztec; *cocoa* and *jerky* (*charqui*) from Quechua; *tattoo* from Tahitian; *thug* from Hindustani; *succotash* from Narraganset; *kimono* from Japanese; and *checkmate* from Arabic.

"Languages may keep the same words, but change their meanings.[14] *Vulgar* used to mean common or popular; now it implies bad. *Awful* meant inspiring with awe; now it is dreadful. Languages change in proportion to the density of communication and the intensity of outside cultural pressures.

The meaning of words reflects the cultural context of the person(s) using the term. A child can define "amen" as meaning "now you can open your eyes." The connotations of words abound in keeping with the cultural influences. If a person seeking a visa to enter another country lists his occupation as *missionary,* he is denied a visa. Yet if he had indicated *pastor* or *preacher,* and better still, *minister,* the visa would have gladly been issued. The problem lies in the cultural association with the term "missionary" that, to many people, implies a superiority/inferiority relationship. There is nothing wrong with the word, but it is difficult to isolate it from the cultural environment.

American English

In the United States, as well as in other countries, such as the Soviet Union, Australia, Latin America, and Ireland, many indigenous languages must have been displaced by intrusive immigrant ones. It must be remembered that English and Spanish are immigrant languages in the United States, vis-à-vis the American Indian languages.

The nature of the migration to America brought people who spoke various languages, although English was predominant. The English imported from England began an evolution of change. Thus American English has a vocabulary that is about 50 percent of German origin and greatly influenced by Latin, French, Spanish, Arabic, and American Indian dialects, in addition to numerous other languages, according to Dr. Eugene Nida, linguist and anthropologist with the American Bible Society. Various sections of the country have intonations and idiosyncrasies that are unique to that segment of the population.

Our nation is a pluralistic society that permits people from every country on the globe to become a participant in a laboratory of intercultural relations. Some predict that, in this land of many languages dominated by American English, the people may be multilingual by AD 2000 because of the influx of people of diverse cultures and languages.

Thus the language usage and the cultural life-style of the people, ethnic groups, is greatly determined by the environment in which they live, work, and associate, as well as in their mobility and desire to relate to their heritages. The ability to discern the effects of these factors in the life of the people will enhance the ability to communicate the gospel to them effectively. This task can best be accomplished with a better understanding of the nature and function of the church.

Channels for Communication

The gospel must be communicated in the cultural context of the hearers and in a language common to their understanding, in the language of their soul, and in the language in which they love and hate. People must hear the gospel in a language they understand. One complication is that many times the speaker may not know if people understand. The innate politeness of most ethnic groups will leave the impression that they understand whether or not they do. Individuals and groups have been known to "make a profession of faith" based purely upon a response of approval by the individual who is speaking, even though they do not understand the spoken message.

Effective communication with language-culture groups and individuals can best be achieved by recognizing the importance of linguistic and cultural factors. These factors may vary widely according to the linguistic and cultural heritage, as well as sociopolitical background of the person.

Communication of the gospel can best be effective by observing these principles:

1. Seek to establish a genuine friendship.
2. Recognize cultural uniqueness.
3. Adapt to the other person's cultural values.
4. Remember, it is a task of reconciliation.
5. Seek to understand similarities, as well as dissimilarities.
6. Establish true communication; if possible, use the person's language.
7. Seek to rewrap the gospel in terms of the new culture.

Thus it becomes imperative that an effective use of the channels of communication, language, and culture, among the various ethnic communities of the nation be utilized to share the love of God through Jesus Christ. If people are to comprehend the significance of a faith relationship with Jesus Christ, it is imperative that it be acknowledged that "faith cometh by hearing and hearing by the word of God" (Rom. 10:17). Thus language and culture are the channels for proclamation of the gospel (Acts 2:5-11).

New Testament Contextual Principles

The uniqueness of America's ethnic diversity calls for basic New Testament principles that are compatible with the complexity of the nation's diversity. Principles are often considered synonymous with methods. Principles are basic and adaptable, while methods are adaptable and constantly changing.

The flexibility to adapt each of the principles to the cultural context and in the language of the people has made it possible for persons to acquire a personal experience with Christ without having to negate their cultural heritage or cross over into another culture. The methodology, techniques, and logistics for the application of these principles are developed on the field locally in keeping with the cultural heritage and context in which the group now lives. The principles, some suggested methods, and selected field experiences are shared in an effort to provide an overview of the contextualization of the biblical message.

These contextual principles must be implemented within the context of each respective ethnic group among whom the gospel is being focused. The principles can be effectively applied with the creative development of methods that are culturally compatible with the continually changing cultural patterns within each particular ethnic group. These methods may need to be implemented in a language other than American English, bilingually, or trilingually. In each instance, the people themselves determine the language usage within their changing cultural patterns.

The application of each principle is distinct. The basic objective of the principle to be applied is considered. The contextual ingredients of each group may be similar; yet these are distinct one from the other. It is suggested that the socioreligious ingredients of the selected ethnic groups be seriously considered. The serious missiologist will want to acquire an overview of the various ethnic categories.

Catalytic missionaries serving in various states among numerous ethnic groups have been responsible for 65-75 percent of the new ethnic congregations each year. Each missionary has planted an average of five new congregations each year, nourished the existing congregations, discovered, enlisted, and trained leaders, et cetera; and yet they work within the framework of the denominational entities. As part of their assigned "homework," the missionaries during the annual Catalytic Missions Conference participate in sharing their field experience related to the application of the contextual church growth principles.

An understanding of the ethnic group among whom the specific principle is to be applied will be helpful in the development of successful approaches in evangelizing ethnic America. The following is a suggested inquiry grid:

Principle

Ethnic Category _____   Ethnic Group _____
Objective: _____
    I. Context—research and describe
       A. Historical background
       B. Language used
       C. Cultural values
          1. Possessions
          2. Pride
          3. Family
          4. Education
          5. Religious background
          6. Time
          7. Food
          8. Fellowship

II. Geographical area where located
   A. Length of time in location
   B. Property status
   C. Permanency
III. Approaches/methods to accomplish task
   A. Approaches
   B. Methods
   C. Techniques

Numerous rereadings of the Book of Acts bring into focus basic fundamental truths that can be applied in sharing the gospel in a changing pluralistic society. The second chapter of Acts lists basic principles for the development of numerous and varied contextual approaches and concepts.

Penetration—Acts 2:41

The context of the selected ethnic group determines the application of the basic penetration principle. Some suggested methods for evangelizing the group are to become acquainted with the cultural heritage of the people; establish friendship with the people, earn the right to be a friend; if possible, become a member of a civic or cultural organization; seek to determine what the people do when they have nothing else to do; visit government entities to become acquainted and offer your talents to help in their projects; seek to initiate a community fellowship to attract groups to discuss the needs of the community from their perspective rather than your point of view; conduct activities for children or youth; use media for spot announcements in the language of the people; secure information and make yourself available to public institutions such as schools, hospitals, jails, and so forth.

A group of Lahu men who had been resettled as refugees in another state came to Visalia, California, seeking a warmer climate. The Lahu tribe originated in China, and part of the tribe migrated to Indochina. People in the community told the missionary that these refugees were in the area. The missionary visited with the men and got acquainted. The local association of Southern Baptist churches and the associational missionary also became interested in helping these men who were skilled in the old-fashioned way of farming in their country. Equipment was secured and on-the-job training began. The men sent word to the group in the other state to join them. Today Visalia is one of two places in the world where the Lahu people live and have the only Baptist church where 300 people worship and study the Bible in their language.

Spiritual Nurture—Acts 2:42-44

Religious heritage and experience determine the application of the principle of spiritual nurture. The development of contextual methods will determine the results of the efforts launched. The following are some suggested methods that have proven effective:

1. Begin with peoples' knowledge of the Bible.
2. Teach biblical truths and basic doctrine.
3. Lead the group to spiritual nurture through biblical teaching and continuous witnessing.
4. Use biblical characters as examples for living.
5. Conduct fellowship events such as Thanksgiving, Christmas, Easter, etc.
6. Use media (e.g., movies, radio, television, to nurture the group).
7. Conduct the meetings in a place conducive to the people. In the beginning be careful not to insist on the people going to the church building.
8. Gradually lead the people in worship experiences.
9. Seek to concentrate on the man who, in ethnic groups, is the head of the house.

Joshua Vang established the Lao congregation as part of the Columbia Drive Baptist Church in Decatur, Georgia. After preaching, Joshua would extend an invitation to those who wanted to profess Christ as their Lord and Savior. However, he did not baptize these persons immediately. The sponsor church could not understand why they would not be baptized in a subsequent service. Joshua had a difficult time getting the Anglo leaders to understand that the people had to have an understanding of the significance of their decision before being baptized. In many instances the people had come forward to express appreciation for what the church had done to help them in resettlement. The persons who had expressed a desire to become Christians were asked to attend an orientation class designed to help them become knowledgeable of the significance of their decisions. After completing the course and again expressing a desire to become a member of the church, the person was baptized.

Use the Language of the People—Acts 2:8

The church must communicate the gospel message, not a new language. The language of the people is basic to evangelization. Some effective methods are suggested below:

1. The use of the language of the people may sometimes call for learning the vernacular spoken every day.
2. The natural leader should be able to communicate in the language of the people.
3. The task of the church is to communicate the gospel rather than teach the classical use of the language.
4. The initiation of classes to help persons learn to read and write in their own language often provides a means of beginning a Bible study group.
5. It may be necessary to use the vernacular to communicate effectively.

The Navajo language is one of the most difficult languages to learn. Few Anglos have acquired the ability to speak it. Years of experience indicated that the task of a non-Navajo person to communicate effectively has often led to various problems that call for their transfer to another field. It is said that during World War II, the United States used the Navajo language to code its messages and the Japanese were never able to break the code.

The work among Navajos "took off" when leaders from among the people responded to God's call, were equipped, and lived contextually. They spoke their language as well as understanding the people.

Economic Ability—Acts 2:44-45

The economic ability and the teaching of biblical steward-ship should determine the type of efforts launched in the growth of the contextual church. Each congregation should be led to become self-sufficient.

Experience indicates that the following methods will lead the congregation to become an autonomous church:

1. Teach, preach, and practice biblical tithing and giving.
2. Every effort should be made to become acquainted with the economic condition in which the people actually live.
3. Respect the group's value of possessions. Plan activities at a time when the group is not deprived of earning their living.
4. Project activities that the group is able to pay for them-selves, (that is, programs, construction of buildings, and so forth).
5. The group should establish their bank account and re-port to the group from the very beginning when offerings are "taken up."
6. Develop a simple budget.
7. Lead the group to accept and exercise financial stability within their economic ability.

The first years of my denominational responsibilities in Texas were in the area of stewardship. During a meeting with the men of one church they agreed to accept total financial responsibility for their pastor's salary. This was a highlight of the week for me. Several weeks later, one of the men who had been present called to share the discussion that they had held among themselves a few days after our meeting. After the initial greeting, he said that the group had asked him to call and express their thoughts. It seems that he had the largest income of any of the members. Yet his income was less than that of the pastor's. The group felt that the worker was worthy of his hire, yet did not see how they could recommend that the church provide a salary in that amount. Mission agencies, in their zeal to provide for the worker, had put the salary above that which the people could and would be willing to pay. The congregation had been "saddled" with an economic burden.

Fellowship—Acts 2:41, 46

Most people enjoy the opportunity of fellowship. Fellowships that are contextual will bring people of like mind and heritage together, thus providing the opportunity for *koinonia* of the believers and the introduction of their friends to the gospel message.

There are numerous methods for applying the principle of fellowship. The following methods have proven effective:

1. Use fellowship events such as picnics, national celebrations, banquets, recognition of community leaders, and others who have achieved a milestone.
2. Operate a booth during the ethnic community events.
3. Recognize the youth of the community as they graduate from high school, receive a scholarship, and so forth.
4. Utilize fellowship to equip leaders.
5. Conduct spiritual enrichment events.
6. Sponsor a baseball, basketball, soccer team.
7. Use the media to announce the events and invite all the community.

Thousands of refugees left Cuba when Fidel Castro became the leader of that country. Often the Baptist churches in the United States held periods of fellowship to share experiences and news of what was happening in Cuba. Through these fellowships, names, addresses, and telephone numbers became available. A large number who came to the fellowships in the early days are members of Baptist churches today.

There are few opportunities for contact among deaf persons. Fellowships provide the people an opportunity to come together with their peers where they can communicate with each other, and so forth. The desire to be with people of kindred minds, language ability, and culture encouraged Southern Baptist deaf persons to travel long distances, at their own expense, to attend the Southern Baptist Conference for the Deaf.

Leaders from Among The People—Acts 2:46

In each ethnic group there are those who are recognized as the leaders of the people. Here are some qualifications that identify the leaders among the people. These factors are:

1. Lives among the people.
2. Speaks the language of the people.
3. Sought out by the people for his guidance.
4. Understands the philosophy and psychology of the life of the people.
5. Has a means of livelihood.
6. Is respected by the people.
7. Has the best education of those identifying with the ethnic group.
8. Is aggressive within the context of the people.

The following methods will help recognize those who are leaders from among the selected ethnic group:

1. Become acquainted with leaders of the ethnic community.

2. Discover the natural leader.
3. Establish a genuine friendship with the natural leader.
4. Evangelize the natural leader, being careful not to isolate him from the people.
5. Equip the natural leader, beginning where he is in his educational achievement. Equip him contextually, lest you isolate him from the people.
6. Give the natural leader opportunities to use his natural talents contextually. (Do not try to emulate him, lest you become unacceptable to the people.)
7. Relinquish the leadership of the group on a gradual basis to the people. This calls for the role of the missionary to decline.

A review of the ethnic/language work indicates that 98 percent of the new churches have been planted by leaders from among the people.

Experiences indicate that, when emphasis is given to encouraging leaders from among the people, the growth of the churches has often doubled, for example, American Indian, Haitian, Arabic, Asian.

The Navajo congregations doubled numerically with the emphasis on seeking, discovering, and equipping Navajo pastors contextually. These men are able to relate to the Navajo Tribal Council in ways and with acceptability previously unknown.

Adequate Facilities—Acts 2:46

Adequate facilities will enhance the effectiveness of methods and other efforts used to evangelize and determine the growth of the church. The facilities should identify, and be owned by, the group.

The selection and usage of the facilities will impact the growth and future of the church. The following methods have proven effective in contextual church growth:

1. Initially begin to meet in familiar surroundings, where the people reside (e.g., a home, rented location, public building, etc.).
2. Use facilities, on a remuneration basis, of an existing church, preferably a church of your own denomination.
3. Begin a building fund almost immediately.
4. Begin looking for a building or site conducive and acceptable to the particular group.
5. Secure your own facilities that are within the financial ability of the group.

Buildings are often designed by persons who have never been to the site. Construction costs are frequently beyond the financial ability of the people. The people receive a grant and a loan and are assured that if they grow and use the latest stewardship plan they will be able to pay off the debt. However, growth is slow, the economy changes, and the debt increases. The people never really get to own the building. The financial burden is larger than the people can carry even if all tithe.

The type of construction should be in the context of the location. For instance, a frame building on eight-foot piling is preferable for use by a Cajun church located in the bayou of Southern Louisiana.

Multiplication—Acts 2:47

Using natural communication channels of the people is most effective in multiplying proclamation of the gospel. Each ethnic group uses its cultural heritage and language to share their experience with relatives, friends, and peers. There is a natural as well as learned channel for multiplication.

The following techniques seek to use natural methods of the people as well as lead them to acquire methods as part of the denomination efforts to carry out the Great Commission:

1. The ethnic "grapevine" provides a means of multiplying naturally.

2. Learn to use the extended family.
3. Use the fellowship meeting to provide a witness.
4. Lead the group to affiliate with a local association.
5. Teach the group to include giving to missions in its first budget.
6. Teach missions, using the Bible as a textbook.
7. Create an awareness of mission opportunities at home and abroad.
8. Lead the group to begin (sponsor) another congregation among another segment of the same ethnic group or another ethnic group.

In 1971 there were two Southern Baptist Korean churches in the United States. I led the Home Mission Board to secure the services of Dr. Dan Y. Moon as a consultant. He is a national church planter and catalyst. Today, there are over seven hundred fifty Korean churches related to the Southern Baptist Convention. The leaders for these churches came from among the people. Although many were Christians before they came to America, only about 5 percent were Baptists prior to arriving in this country.

The Korean pastors organized themselves into a national fellowship. They soon became aware that large numbers of Koreans were migrating to South America. Having decided to plant churches in South America, they were encouraged to work within the financial plan of the denomination. In a discussion held in Los Angeles in 1985 with the leaders of the Foreign Mission Board, the Koreans learned that it would not be possible to accomplish their commitment through the denominational channels. They began to explore ways of evangelizing Koreans in other nations. Today, there are Korean Baptist churches in South America, the USSR, North Korea, and Northern China. American Korean youth have established American English-speaking churches in various cities and are in turn establishing Korean language churches for their parents.

The use of contextual principles in church planting and in church development have proven to be effective in contextualization of the biblical message. These principles provide the basis for deculturalizing the biblical message. They also provide the flexibility to creatively develop methodology and materials that are relevant to the various segments of Americans who live in changing cultural patterns.

1. E.C. Watson, *Superintendent of Missions of An Association* (Atlanta: Home Mission Board, 1969), "Foreword."

2. F. Michael Novak, *The Rise of the Unmeltable Ethnic* (New York: MacMillan Co., 1972), 35.

3. George Arthur Butttrick, ed., *The Interpreters Dictionary of the Bible* (Nashville and New York: Abingdon Press, 1962), vol. 3, 67.

4. Merrill C. Tenney, *The Zondervan Pictorial Encyclopedia of the Bible* (Grand Rapids: Zondervan Publishing House, 1975), vol. 5, 847.

5. Ibid., 845.

6. Ibid., Buttrick, vol. 1, 608.

7. H. H. Hobbs, *Fundamentals of Our Faith,* (Nashville: Broadman Press, 1960), 125.

8. Stephen Thernstorm, *Harvard Encyclopedia of American Ethnic Groups* (Cambridge: Harvard University, Belknap Press, 1980), 782.

9. Oscar I. Romo, "A Southern Baptist Perspective of Hispanic Missions" (Atlanta: Home Mission Board, 1982), unpublished paper, 24.

10. Michael Novak, *The Rise of the Unmeltable Ethnics* (New York: MacMillan, 1972), 47.

11. Oscar I. Romo, "Back to the Future" (Atlanta: Home Mission Board, 1988), unpublished paper, 8.

12. Paul G. Hiebert, *Cultural Anthropology* (Philadelphia: J.B. Lippincott Co., 1976), 276.

13. Eugene A. Nida, *Customs and Cultures,* (Pasadena: William Carey Library, 1975), 209.

14. Nida, 209.

4 Contextualization

Before the world was created, the Word already existed; he was with God, and he was the same as God. From the very beginning the Word was with God. Through him God made all things; not one thing in all creation was made without him. The Word was the source of life, and this life brought light to mankind (John 1:1-4, GNB).

Frequently, the typical church, in its efforts to include everyone in its congregation, unconsciously practices "Manifest Destiny." The church's insistence is more of an effort to appease its conscience, since historically it has ministered primarily to those of "its own kind." In its efforts to be all inclusive, the church launches programs to "Americanize" rather than "evangelize," often saying, "let them be part of us."

The majority of ethnic people becomes aware that methodology and language usage represent an effort to subconsciously implement the melting-pot concept, and they resist the well-intended efforts. Besides, when ethnics do attend church, they often have no idea of what is going on nor do they feel at ease in an environment where they are recognized as being different from the predominant group.

Often context is erroneously defined as geographical and numerical. In reality, it also includes the history of the ethnic group, language usage, cultural values, religious experience, economics, education, social structure, political aspects, et cetera. An awareness of the fabric that comprises the specific group makes possible the weaving of the gospel message into the life of the people.

The church, in essence, reflects the experiences, expressions, and witness of its members in their relationships with God in their own sociocultural settings, in forms, and through structures which are appropriate to that context.[1] Therefore, the gospel must be shared within the context of the people.

Context, derived from the Latin *contexere*, refers to the weaving together of various dimensions of life. Human life consists of cultural, social, historical, linguistic, economic, and political dimensions that are under constant change by new influences.[2] Language and culture become the vehicles through which various influences are woven into the constantly changing lives of people in a pluralistic society. The contextualization of the gospel means all that is implied in "indigenization;" and yet it seeks to press beyond.[3] John L. Nevins, in the *Indigenization of the Korean Church*, established these principles, among others:

1. To let each man abide in the calling wherein he was found, teaching that each was to be an individual at work for Christ in his neighborhood.
2. To develop . . . methods and machinery only as far as the native church was able to care and manage them.[4]

According to G. Linwood Barney, professor at the Alliance School of Theology, context, indigenization, is "disengaging the supracultural elements of the gospel from one culture to another and contextualizing them within the cultural forms and social institutions of another, with at least some degree of transformation of those forms and institutions."[5] The church must be equipped to deal with the rapid social change, diverse cultural patterns in a pluralistic society, and forms of institutionalized Christianity. "Although Christianity must be a life-giving and life-changing force in a culture, it does not necessarily have to be a foreign element in the sense of being identified with another culture."[6] The gospel must be recognizable to people within their cultural matrices.

Communication is a prime dynamic that determines the kind and rate of exchange in society.[7] It involves relationships, an exchange of energy, challenges the individual beyond the status quo, provides new insights, and new attitudes toward people. Communication is an agent of change that alters relationships between the minority group and the majority group. In a sense, each person/group adapts or relinquishes some of tradition in an effort to exchange ideas and/or concepts, such as the concept of God.

Contextual communication is the logic by which symbols and words are connected. Human communication is achieved by means of expressive actions which operate as signals, signs, and symbols. The Christian's goal in "communication has always been to present the supracultural message of the gospel in culturally relevant terms."[8]

Creation and Culture

"God made all things through His Word."[9] God spoke and the world came into existence. The land and living beings are reflections of the substance of God's word. The words conceived in God's mind are communicated to man whom God created in His image. By creating mankind, God, in effect, created cultures now perceived in a variety of ways.

Old Testament

The Ten Commandments provide the basis for a God-human relationship. The first four Commandments (Ex. 20:1-11) deal with God and worship regularly. The other six Commandments (vv. 12-17) refer to human relationships. These relationship codes have been, in a sense, the basis for mankind throughout the world manifested in specific behavioral patterns. Cultural diversity found in the world is but a beautiful expression of the way God created humanity with a propensity for variety.

Sin was, and is, the basis for the human dethroning of the Creator and enthroned creation as an object of worship. These beliefs confuse and frustrate people today. This led to the development of various religious systems.

The Old Testament gives attention to three cultural factors. Ancient social structures were based on personal kinships and group interaction. The twelve sons of Jacob fathered the twelve tribes of Israel. God's interaction with people is the primary topic of the Bible. God called Abram. Abram listened to God and obeyed in faith. The Scriptures mention Abram as the individual through whom "all nations will be blessed" (Gen. 12:3). The Scriptures are filled with relational information and genealogies. The genealogies establish the validity of Jesus but the entire New Testament is based upon the truth of the Old Testament.

Human organization into twelve tribes was the establishment of a cultural system. People of a kinship culture developed interactive patterns among themselves as well as with others. In establishing the Mosaic law, God explicated the means of behavioral control. The function of law gradually developed into a political organization. These principles are much the same; their application is global rather than regional.

New Testament

Anticipating human weakness, God put His plan into effect. Only through an individual such as Christ, who had a pre-fall relationship with God, could there be restoration of the potential humanity had lost.

The apostle Paul wrote in Ephesians 1:4, 8-10,

> Even before the world was made, God had already chosen us to be his through our union with Christ, so that we would be holy and without fault before him. In all his wisdom and insight God did what he had purposed, and made known to us the

secret plan he had already decided to complete by means of Christ. This plan, which God will complete when the time is right, is to bring all creation together, everything in heaven and on earth, with Christ as head (GNB).

The implementation of the discovery principle was central to Jesus' communication of the truth. Jesus encouraged people to experience/demonstrate by challenging people to discover the truth by using appropriate cultural standards; and when cultural standards were not appropriate, He demonstrated where culture was wrong. Thus Jesus used language and culture as channels for communicating with mankind.

The New Testament presents various sets of human circumstances. First, it describes Christ's coming and the completion of His salvific work. Second, it describes the missionary expansion of the church as well as the instruments used in that outreach. There are several instances in which our attention is focused on the reports of individuals such as Paul, Peter, and the Ethiopian eunuch. The New Testament shares the evidence of tension as the early believers struggled to make the transition to other cultures. Here are some encounters: 1. Politics (Acts 16:19-40); 2. Religion and philosophy (Acts 17:16-34); 3. Magic (Acts 13:4-12); 4. Economics (Acts 19:23-41).

Each of the Gospels reflects the cultural orientation of its author and is addressed to a particular audience. Also, the church leaders sought "to establish a basis for an ongoing contextualization working systematically to eliminate a number of obstacles both within and without the church."[10] Peter and Paul are reported to have struggled with issues (Gal. 2:11-16) similar to those resolved at the Jerusalem Council (Acts 15).

"The transition to contextualization as we know it today did not begin until the New Testament era."[11]

God, through Christ, chose not to be separated from culture. He chose through Christ to become involved and work (as a human being) in human affairs. "Christ was the epitome of this incarnation style of communication."[12] Jesus interacted with the world.

God, through language and culture, communicates into reality the same message into the context of the modern receptor.

Contextual Church Growth

Experience as a missionary, pastor, and denominational employee made me aware of the need for principles that could pragmatically be applied among all the language-culture groups. This endeavor led to the study of various Southern Baptist "principles" which, in reality, are Southern-cultural and rural-oriented methods. Consultations were held with missiologists, missions professors, anthropologists, theologists, and numerous other authorities in the United States and in several foreign countries. In each instance, there were things to learn and to discard. It seemed that almost every idea or suggestion was focused at the foreign mission field, with almost no attention to the reality of the ethnicity of our own nation. I embarked upon extensive reading and research related to a variety of disciplines as well as the Bible.

The Book of Acts written by the physician Luke to "Theophilus," friend of God, records the last words of Jesus that are known as the Great Commission: "You will be witnesses for me in Jerusalem, in all of Judea and Samaria, and to the ends of the earth" (Acts 1:8, GNB). Acts records the experiences of sharing the gospel among the Gentiles. "The Lord has never intended for the gospel message of Jesus to remain *bottled up* in one culture."[13] Acts traces important events in the history of the early church, and the outpouring of the Holy Spirit, beginning in Jerusalem.

After appearing to the disciples for forty days (Acts 1:3), the Lord tells them to wait in Jerusalem for the fulfillment of His promise. In expectancy, the believers opened the vertical window of their souls—*pneuma*—and felt a "breath of fresh air," the Holy Spirit empowering them to "go forth" in their task of fulfilling the Great Commission.

The power is to be given in such times and in such measures as should appear best to the infinite wisdom of God. God was "urging them to go beyond what they had known both of geography and culture to see the universal implications of the gospel."[14] The Great Commission demonstrates the fact of the universality of the gospel, that God's gracious salvation is for all mankind in Christ. Acts shares the experiences of the Gentile Christians as Christianity spread from Jerusalem to Rome.

The gospel of Jesus Christ is to be taught to all nations—*ta ethne* (Matt. 28:19). "The gospel is to be adapted to all the varying minds and habits of men, barbarous and civilized, near and remote, ignorant or cultivated; . . . and make it known in all quarters of the globe."[15] The church in the twentieth century is "challenged to communicate the gospel, given in a cultural setting and pertinent to that setting, into another cultural context and to make it relevant to the individual in that setting."[16]

First Church-Growth Conference

The Book of Acts contains the proceedings of the first "church-growth conference" held in Jerusalem. It seems that the church in Jerusalem had heard of the "evaluation" of the message being preached throughout Asia Minor, that required the keeping of the Mosaic law (15:1). Paul and Barnabas were recalled to Jerusalem to appear before the apostles and elders (v. 2). Paul and Barnabas testified on the return trip among the Gentiles (v. 3).

A council was summoned to deal with the "big question." Could the Gentiles—ethnics—become Christians while retaining their cultural heritage or did they have to become Jews—Anglos—to be Christians?

Upon their arrival in Jerusalem, Paul and Barnabas appeared before the council to present their report (v. 4). A debate was held as to the acculturalization of the gospel by inclusion of the Mosaic law as an essential to salvation (vv. 5-6). Peter arose and addressed the council indicating that salvation was by faith and not by works (vv. 7-11). Paul and Barnabas were then asked to speak before the council as to the miracles and wonders that God had worked among the Gentiles (v. 12). James arose to address the council indicating that they should not trouble those from among the Gentiles who were turning to God, but that they should be encouraged to abstain from idols, immorality, and so forth (v. 13-21).

The council sent a letter to the Gentiles stating, "The Holy Spirit and we have agreed not to put any other burden on you besides these necessary rules: eat no food that has been offered to idols; eat no blood; eat no animal that has been strangled; and keep yourselves from sexual immorality" (vv. 28-29, GNB).

George R. Beasley-Murray states it:

> The result of the controversy was that it settled once and for all the basic question whether Gentiles became Christian by way of Judaism. The direction of the Christian mission was definitely set by God in the home of a Roman centurion, and Jesus Christ brought the first of the Gentile families into the redeemed fellowship when He gave His spirit to a Roman.

The decision of the Jerusalem Council affirmed unity in diversity. Gentiles who were circumcised would have crossed cultural lines and thus not been able to be Christians within their own cultural context. Christianity would have remained a small Jewish sect.

We can affirm unity in diversity when we adapt our methodology to the needs of the various ethnic groups, while at the same time finding a sense of unity in our commitment to proclaim the gospel to every creature.

Culturally-Informed Theology

A culturally-informed theology provides a positive view of the other person's culture. While it is true that all cultures have elements in them that come under the judgment of God, there are many aspects of culture that can be appreciated.

Contextual church growth is the result of a culturally-informed theology that helps us:

1. Develop a positive attitude toward other cultures.
2. Adapt the gospel to the cultural context.
3. Permit diversity without threatening our unity.
4. Use culture as a channel that permits the gospel to be communicated in the language of the people.

The church can be composed of distinct groups, each with its own identity and each group sharing its identity with Jesus Christ. This was the recognition of homogeneous units (local churches) within the church, universal. Wherever Paul lingered to preach the gospel, a local church was established and developed. Each was a local church, with distinct identities—cultural and perhaps even linguistic. Each differed in "color," yet were the same. There was diversity within unity, in the New Testament church, as recorded in Acts.

The era of the professional minister and the European-culture church in America is coming to an end. Often, people in leadership and academic positions have indicated that, to establish a Southern Baptist church in a particular community, one gathers all the Southern Baptists and starts a church. In the height of the civil-rights movement there were churches that had to change their by-laws to admit those who were not Caucasian. These churches were, and are, in reality cultural "clubs." People sought out the church. The denomination and the minister focused on programs that were "uniform" for use within the church. Many of the best-trained ministers are reaching a point of moderate success, only to gradually become aware that the familiar way of ministry is no longer effective. The day of the "typical, traditional, Anglo-oriented" church is coming to an end. Southern Baptists who went west and north are now retiring and returning "home" to spend their last days among friends. The churches they established in the urban areas in the North and West are declining. Often, the typical answer is to provide a greater emphasis to rural-oriented methods. Unfortunately the prescription for a declining church is "take two of these and call me in the morning."

"Cultural myopia" has set in and these staunch proclaimers of the faith have yet to realize that the "American melting pot" is a myth. Through the years, these "compassionate believers" have established friendships with ethnic people, enjoyed ethnic meals, learned selected non-English phrases, and even invited the ethnics to their homes and to "our church." It has been assumed that the ethnic wants to be "like us" and prefers to speak American English. The truth is that the American mission field is now ethnic and will intensify in its ethnicity.

Empowered to Proclaim

Dependence on the Holy Spirit's power and leadership is essential to all church planting. This is especially true in cultivating and harvesting in a continuing ministry. "But you shall receive [miraculous] power [*ouvauis;* strength] when the Holy Spirit has come upon you; and you shall be My witnesses both in Jerusalem, and in all Judea and Samaria, and even to the remotest [uttermost] part of the earth" (Acts 1:8, NASB). This is the third time Luke gave a definite promise of the risen Lord to His disciples.

The disciples were to be witnesses or instruments in proclaiming the good news of Christ. In commissioning the disciples, Jesus urged them to go beyond their knowledge of geography and culture. The Spirit came upon the God-fearing Greeks in Caesarea. Cornelius, a Gentile centurion, and his companions experienced the power of the Spirit (Acts 10:44-48). Luke wrote in Acts the experiences of the Gentiles as Christianity moved out from Jerusalem to Rome.

Ethnic church planting is done in obedience to the Great Commission, "Go . . . make disciples of all nations," *ta ethne*

(Matt. 28:19). Obedience to the call of Christ is to give of themselves, dedicate their lives as proclaimers of the gospel. Each person goes empowered by the Holy Spirit who provides guidance, opens doors, and watches over them. The twentieth-century disciples have been empowered to proclaim the gospel among ethnic Americans.

Courts Shepard had been selected to serve as a catalytic missionary in San Diego, California. Placed to serve in a difficult setting, tolerated, but not necessarily accepted by the local structure, he found it difficult to penetrate the community. Courts sought God's leadership and guidance in accomplishing the task. One day as he walked down the street he felt compelled to cross the street. Within a block, he noticed a man walking toward him. Courts approached the man, shared the biblical message in simple terms, and the man became a Christian. A few weeks later Courts discovered that the new Christian had at his fingertips the ability to contact the ethnic communities in the city.

Thirteen months after obeying God's command to go to San Diego, Courts had planted eighteen congregations and led 150 people to Christ.

Don Kim came to the United States from Korea to study at the Massachusetts Institute of Technology. Responding to God's call, Don graduated from seminary and moved to Los Angeles to serve among Koreans. Don's vision and commitment laid the foundation for the Korean church planting emphasis under the leadership of Dan Y. Moon. In 1971 there were two Korean churches; today there are more than seven hundred and fifty.

José S. Flores, a pioneer of Hispanic work in Texas, continued to serve as pastor of the church in San Marcos, and became an itinerant missionary. As the people followed the harvesting of crops, he followed the people. José, in his lifetime, planted at least one hundred and fifty churches in Texas and other states and encouraged numerous men to respond to God's call to Christian service.

The Book of Acts concludes with Paul, "preaching the kingdom of God and teaching about the Lord Jesus Christ quite openly and unhindered" (Acts 28:31, RSV). The Spirit of God continues to work among the twentieth-century disciples who hear His voice and commit themselves to carry out the Great Commission.

Contextual Concepts

Life is a series of learning experiences. As a child, I knew by experience that the melting-pot concept was a myth, a lie! Life on the street, in the theater, in school, and even in church indicated that all were supposedly equal. However, some were more equal than others.

The evangelical church where our family attended tried to emulate our "model" church; the Anglo church on whom the congregation depended. Unfortunately, the model by which the Spanish congregation was to measure its growth, life, et cetera was more of a cultural club and, in the opinion of many, did not resemble the model church, the New Testament church. It seemed that the emphasis was on Americanization rather than evangelization. The achievement of the American dream was predominant in their efforts regardless of the consequences experienced by their "Christian brothers." Yet my personal experiences and acquaintance with biblical teachings since childhood indicated that the gospel is for all people everywhere, regardless of language usage and cultural heritage. People need not negate a rich language and cultural heritage to become a Christian.

Concept(s) are "a prominent aspect of human thought processes (ideas) that develop slowly through experience and are used to represent a diversity of particular objectives and events."[17] Concepts are learning systems; their transformation makes the "idea" socioculturally relevant and capable of facing the challenge of communicating the biblical message in the ethnolinguistic context of the particular ethnic group. Ethnic church growth concepts are the result of forty years of experience in working among numerous ethnic groups, on the reservation, in rural, village, and urban settings, and in state, national, and international settings.

These concepts provide the opportunity for expression, creativity, thought, participation, implementation, and evaluation of the various programs which are essential in the development of a viable strategy focused at people living in changing ethnic patterns.

Ethnic Church Planting

Laser Church Growth Thrust

The magnitude of the task of evangelizing the nation's ethnic population calls for imagination, exercise of values, attitudes, feelings, convictions, and aspirations that actually transcend the cognitive domain of those seeking to carry out the command of Christ—"Go...tell." The Laser Thrust concept seeks to penetrate, cultivate, motivate, and establish (plant) new ethnic/language work, strengthen existing churches, and develop a long-range strategy with a minimum investment of resources, human and financial.

LASER is an acronym for *Light Amplification by Stimulated Emission of Radiation*. The laser pumps light into a ruby crystal. When the atoms of the ruby crystal are illuminated, they pick up excess energy. The energy is discharged in the form of a light beam—thus the laser beam. This beam has many uses: radar tracking, range finding, welding, cutting steel at great distances, surgery—"mend a retina"—magnifying to three dimensions, and penetration.

The laser beam projects active materials (light waves) that can be amplified in density and focused so as to travel in a single direction, tuned to a fine point, or spread over a wide area. Laser Thrust focuses the components of witness in the penetration of selected areas—whether village or urban areas—in beginning new work. Its methods are simple, adaptable, and flexibly developed within the cultural system of the target group.

Persons with experience and knowledge of the language and culture of the target group(s) are thrust into the area for a short period of time (three days to a week). They seek to locate the targeted persons, establish communication with them, share their experiences in the Lord, lead those people to a personal relationship with Christ, and establish a new work. The natural leaders are sought out from among the people, and the new work is related to existing works for spiritual nurture and equipping of leaders.

Paul, the apostle, led the penetrating, cultivating, motivating, and planting of new churches in the first century—Acts 9–12. The Laser Thrust is an ethnic church-growth concept that seeks to focus on these objectives in a twentieth-century microcosmic/pluralistic society.

A Laser Thrust Guide has been designed to assist churches in their efforts to share the gospel of Jesus Christ with ethnic/language-culture persons, especially in the urban areas.

Los Angeles Laser

The Laser Thrust in 1977 focused on sixteen ethnic groups. Twenty-two ethnic groups were contacted, and ten new congregations were planted. Twenty-two places were prioritized for new work.

A Language Church Growth Strategy was designed. The metro area was mapped into regions, both geographically and culturally. The strategy called for thirty-nine new personnel; however, funds were available for only two. A cycling approach was designed for future catalytic personnel. Priorities were established for the next twenty-five years. Between 1979 and 1984 seventy-five new language congregations were planted.

The Laser strategy design developed in 1977, with a few changes, is still relevant in the 1990s.

Houston Laser

The penetration planning targeted eighteen ethnic groups. Twenty-two groups were contacted. Twelve new congregations were planted. Projections for twenty-two additional groups were planned. Between 1979-84, a total of seventy-five new congregations were established in keeping with the strategy and priorities planned during the Laser.

Catalytic Church Growth

Catalytic church growth, an ethnic church-growth concept, is New Testament in origin.

In science, catalytic agents are injected into various types of settings. Because of their consistency and presence, these agents cause reactions that, in turn, become actions that influence the makeup, consistency, looks, and uses of the setting penetrated by the catalytic agent. The catalytic agent maintains its equilibrium and stability; thus being able to function and influence its new surroundings.

The catalytic church growth concept calls for sensitivity, creativity, and accelerated action in the proclamation of the biblical message. The gospel is injected into the natural setting of the people, using available resources and transforming the lives of the people. These efforts will result in the development of indigenous churches in the ethnolinguistic context of the people.

Paul, the apostle, was the first catalytic missionary. Led by the Holy Spirit, he went as directed by God. He spoke words of wisdom, taught with authority, related the message to the natural setting of the people, and caused changes that brought a spiritual experience in the lives of many (see 1 Cor. 2:13).

The gospel seed was sown wherever Paul went. His missionary journeys show he established churches, sought out leaders, equipped the people to serve, and continued in the task as catalyst (3:6).

His experience on the road to Damascus was the basis for Paul's commitment; a commitment that called for work, flexibility, creativity, and stability as he faced the world of his day (4:10-15).

The task of cultivation was perhaps the most difficult for Paul. This task was to tenderly remove the weeds, plant churches, and watch the churches develop as he encouraged, and watered their growth; a growth that was natural to the setting in which the churches were located (3:7).

Paul, the servant, sought to minister by seeking out and enlisting leaders, equipping them to serve, guiding their efforts, encouraging their maturity, and prayerfully undergirding them (4:1-7).

The catalytic church-growth concept was initiated in 1965. This concept has been effectively used among Hispanics, Indians, Arabs, Asians, Caribbeans, Europeans, and so forth.

The growth of the Hispanic work is due largely to leadership from among the people as well as the development of materials. American Indians have grown as they have sought to do things the Indian way, led by Indian leaders. The growth of work among Arabs and Koreans is due largely to leaders who understand the language and culture of those people and share their natural identity.

The catalytic missionary seeks to penetrate and plant churches in the ethnolinguistic community—be it linguistic, cultural, or geographical.

The initiation of new work or the revitalization of existing groups calls for the catalyst to be creative and flexible in examining and suggesting various approaches or methods to meet the needs of the people.

The catalyst seeks out potential natural leaders, equips them for service, assists as called upon, guides their work without "controlling" them, serves as a friend, and prayerfully undergirds them.

Developing methods relevant to various ethnic groups calls for creativity. These methods must be based upon sound church-growth principles and in keeping with the group's ability to implement them. The correlation of the development of each church in its natural/contextual setting is essential for the growth of indigenous churches.

Often it becomes necessary to develop and/or adapt contextual language materials for the various uses on the field served. Thus the catalyst should stay aware of current materials.

The vision of missionary opportunities should constantly be shared with the people of God. These opportunities are for reaching nearby communities, as well as the entire world, as part of the denomination.

The catalytic missionary should be a pragmatic individual with a commitment to God to "share the Word" and a leader who is creative, flexible, sensitive, patient with personal fortitude, cooperative, and visionary.

The catalytic church growth concept permits the development of indigenous churches whose growth is greatly determined by our vision, philosophy, and commitment to the task.

Catalytic Missions

The catalytic missionary seeks to bring ethnic/language-culture persons in the designated areas into a right relationship with Christ and to develop indigenous churches in the ethnolinguistic context of the people.

Responsibilities

1. Initiates and guides the beginning of new work/church planting.
2. Assists churches in state/region to develop aggressive ethnic/language-culture programs.
3. Creatively discovers new mission methods.

4. Selects, trains, assists, and guides laypersons and lay preachers to serve voluntarily in new work efforts.
5. Develops materials for use in leadership training of ethnic/language-culture persons.
6. Develops contextual language materials designed to assist the development of contextually autonomous churches.
7. Participates with others in implementing training opportunities of ethnic/language-culture persons.
8. Provides guidance to churches in state/region in meeting the mission opportunities.
9. Presents missions as requested but without interference with the work assigned.
10. Cooperates with the associational and denominational emphasis giving special attention to relating the congregations to both.
11. Accepts other assignments as requested by mission agencies.

First Romanian Baptist Church, Chicago

Pastor Valentin Popovici calls; his strong voice sings out the ancient words of faith and hope: "Hristos a înviat!" and the congregation responds as one, "Adevărt c-a înviat!" The resurrection message, "Christ is risen," is incredibly good news to the grateful assembly—a cross section of Romanian political refugees and immigrants.

The church was founded in 1970 by the senior pastor, Alexa Popovici, Valentin's father. The 700-member church occupies an aging building on one of Chicago's major thoroughfares. It is the spiritual and cultural center for Romanian Baptists in Chicago. "Our culture prohibits going house to house to evangelize," says Pastor Valentin. The church uses other methods: special services at Easter, Christmas, choir concerts, and children's programs with recitation, poetry, and music, as drawing cards. Its weekly radio program provides an entry into homes.

Persons coming from Romania have said that they heard the program by shortwave in their home country.

The church has provided the vision, support, and leadership for Romanian work in Seattle, San Francisco, Los Angeles, Houston, Akron, Atlanta, Philadelphia, and other cities, thus multiplying itself in a natural contextual manner.

America's Arabs

Khalil "Charlie" Hanna, a catalytic missionary among Middle Easterners, is the spiritual father for many Arab American Christians. In fourteen years, Hanna has planted forty congregations, discovered natural leaders, written Bible study and other materials, secured meeting places, and directed the Ethnic Leadership Development Center in Riverside. Twenty-four of the congregations planted have survived.

Today there are seventy Arabic-speaking congregations in the Southern Baptist Convention among Chadians, Egyptians, Jordanians, Iraqis, Kuwaitis, Syrians, Palestinians, Lebanese, Saudis, Sudanese, and Yemenites. These congregations meet wherever they can—homes, rented facilities, and in the buildings of other churches. Hanna's dream is for one of the Arabic congregations to have their own building. Charlie smiles and ends the conversation saying, "God will give the Arabs a building!"

Kaleidoscopic Church Growth

The kaleidoscope is an instrument containing loose bits of colored glass between two plates and two plane mirrors. Changes of position of the bits of glass reflect an endless variety of patterns. The glass in the instrument remains the same; the change is in its arrangement. Change is caused by an outside force.

The unchangeable elements of the kaleidoscopic church are: 1. Proclamation of Jesus Christ; 2. Worship; 3. Leadership development; 4. Ministering effectively; 5. Missions.

This concept permits the church to serve a mobile, transitional, and/or ethnolinguistic setting. Basic to this concept is the opportunity for Christian expression that varies from culture to culture. The leaders identify with the people, since the leaders come from among the people. It communicates in the language of the community. The organizational structure must be suited to meet the needs of the community. It identifies with and serves the people in the community, providing a natural witness that reproduces new congregations.

The kaleidoscopic church grows in a variety of life-styles, economic variances, educational levels, racial tensions, linguistic channels, cultural uniquenesses, geographical barriers, and living conditions. It replaces the transitional church, which serves only people in a given setting. It permits various groups to work cooperatively, yet the people retain their identity, language, and cultural uniqueness.

New Testament church growth principles are inherent in its basic but changing and multiple contexts. It ministers to the spiritual and social needs of the people where its facilities are located. Its flexibility and uniqueness permit the kaleidoscopic church to multiply itself in one or more settings.

In a sense, the kaleidoscopic concept calls for the formation of a conglomerate of churches, somewhat similar to a multinational corporation. This conglomerate would provide for joint ownership, cooperative operation, and fellowship of churches that seek to serve all the people in the community. Each church elects members to the board of directors of the corporation. The operation costs are prorated to each church on a prearranged basis. The board determines the use of facilities, owns the buildings, and so forth. Thus, each group feels ownership and responsibility for usage and maintenance. In the event one of the churches decides to move, it can "sell" its stock in the corporation. To begin a new congregation within the facilities, the stock is split and the new group becomes a partner in the corporation.

Each church is autonomous (not departments, satellites, etc.), has its own pastor, budget, deacons, programs, and activities as it may determine. The pastor of each church serves on the minister's council of the corporation with the intent of seeking to meet the needs of the community. The council selects its chairman on a rotating basis, thereby insuring that every pastor has a leadership role.

Each church has its own pastor. The pastors meet on a regular schedule to discuss working cooperatively. The group selects its leader by an agreed-upon basis. In an urban area, the pastor of one of the churches visits for all of the churches, not just for the one for which he is responsible. Theoretically, the family members in a home would attend the church of their choice. For example, the family consists of an Anglo father, a Korean mother, and their children. The father attends the English language church; the mother the Korean church; and the children select the church of their choice. The Golden West Worship Center in Westminster, California, in essence, seeks to best project the idea of the Kaleidoscopic Church Growth Concept.

The First Baptist Church of Westminster, California was founded by Southerners who moved to California. According to the records, it had 2,392 members and large, unused facilities; they could only locate 190 members living in the area. Seeking a way to keep the old property while helping to start new congregations, the pastor began to develop "cluster congregations," which gradually emerged as autonomous churches. This gives validity to the Kaleidoscopic Church Growth Concept.

Golden West Worship Center is an umbrella for six churches—Anglo, Vietnamese, Korean, Japanese, Spanish, Messianic Hebrew—plus a deaf group that gathers in one building. Each is an autonomous church and contributes to the operation of the facilities. Each church provides members the opportunity to worship in their language and cultural context without giving up their identity.

Sponsorship

The Book of Acts indicated that new churches were started almost spontaneously as Spirit-led men and women witnessed in various places and new believers came together for fellowship, to study the Scriptures, for worship, prayer, and mutual support. "The Holy Spirit worked to create a community of believers."[18]

The church in Jerusalem experienced great growth. People were saved and baptized. Leaders were developed from among the people. Stephen, having been one of the seven chosen as "deacons," ventured out and began to witness and preach in the synagogues. Stephen was not an emissary of the Jerusalem church but an individual following the leadership of the Holy Spirit. Neither was Philip an emissary officially sponsored by the church. Only after Philip's success in evangelizing Samaritans did the apostles take notice and send Peter and John to investigate and "validate" Philip's activities. Peter received his commission from God in a vision to visit Cornelius. The Jerusalem believers, namely those originally from Cyprus and Cyrene, traveled as far as Antioch of Syria and began to witness to the Hellenists (Greek-speaking Jews who had adopted varying degrees of Greek culture).

The church in Jerusalem, upon hearing of what the Lord was doing, responded by sending Barnabas to assist. Although the church had not initiated nor sponsored the new work, they indicated a readiness and willingness to assist in the growth and development of these new churches.

The early Baptist history of America indicates an active involvement of Baptists in outreach following the same pattern as the apostle Paul. Paul and Barnabas, having been released from their responsibilities at the church in Jerusalem, were led by the Holy Spirit on their first missionary journey. Paul established churches and appointed elders in every church (Acts 3–4; 14:23). The churches consisted of believers who were Hellenistic Jews and Gentiles of diverse cultures.

Sponsorship as a church planting concept emerged when Baptist families who had traveled to Texas and established "stations" (missions) requested support from the Home Mission Board and Georgia Baptists. These two entities became the supporters of the first missionary to arrive in Texas, who constituted the First Baptist Church in Galveston. Sponsorship of missions (stations) and churches in today's approach began to emerge in the 1930s. By 1951 Solomon Dowis noted in his book, *O Jerusalem, Our Cities for Christ,* that the sponsorship concept is fairly well accepted. "A... better way to establish new churches is for the local church to select a needy field and establish the new work through its own leadership.... This method... gives experienced leadership, denominational relationship, encouragement, and fellowship to the new church."[19] In 1956 C. C. Warren, president of the Southern Baptist Convention, challenged the denomination to sponsor the 30,000 Movement.

Sponsorship in the latter part of the twentieth century should be contextual, especially the effort to plant new ethnic churches. The sponsor church should provide an identity, lend its leaders in the initial years, teach and lead in planning within the context of the people, guide the group of new believers— without smothering them—to develop their own leadership, grow in doctrinal stability, denominational loyalty, evangelistic efforts, missionary outreach, and other endeavors that would enhance the work of the kingdom. The sponsor should be aware that they are not the "bishop" over the ethnic congregation but a brother helping a brother. Leadership can best be provided through fellowship. The mission congregation should handle its own finances with the sponsor assisting and guiding, but permitting the group to develop as stewards. The facilities which the sponsor provides the "mission" for its use should be given to the congregation on the day of its organization into a church.

The mission congregation should be led and encouraged to

organize as a church. To do otherwise will result in "smother-ship" rather than sponsorship. "Churches reproduce themselves as new churches."[20] Sponsorship is the relationship of equals; equals before God helping each other to carry out the Great Commission to go into all the world.

The First Chinese Southern Baptist Church in Los Angeles sponsored a new congregation in Sacramento, 400 miles away. Laypersons from the church traveled to Sacramento each week to lead in the development of the First Chinese Southern Baptist Church of Sacramento.

The American Korean Baptist Church in Chicago, whose members are American-born Koreans and prefer to speak American English, sponsored a Korean-language congregation for their parents.

Concern for ethnics led a large church to sponsor several satellite congregations. However, the church would not permit these to organize into churches, lest it lose members.

A black church in California sponsored a Hispanic congregation.

A Korean church in California sponsored an Anglo congregation.

The Greek church in Toronto, Canada, sponsored a Greek congregation in Boston.

A strong Anglo church saw the need to establish an ethnic church among a particular group. The church worked through its Missions Development Council and the Associational Development Council to determine the procedure for starting the new church. A location was found, and the decision was made to purchase the property. A leader was found.

A core group was brought together. Together with the sponsoring church, guidelines and procedures were set up for handling the funds. The relationship of the mission members to the sponsoring church was established. Clear guidelines on the use of the facilities of the sponsoring church were delineated. After a brief time, the mission was organized as a church, given the original property, along with a newly built facility to meet current and future needs. Pulpit exchanges and shared celebrations merged and strengthened the two congregations. Both churches grew.

Refugee Church Growth
Sojourners: Biblical Perspective

The late President John F. Kennedy said, "There is no part of our nation that has not been touched by our immigrant background. Everywhere immigrants have enriched and strengthened the fabric of American life."[21]

"Almost the entire history of the migration of the Hebrew Jewish people falls into three grand chapters: the Exodus, the Exile, and the Dispersion. In large, part of the Jews became refugees for conscience sake, although other factors, both political and economic, played a part."[22]

Abraham became a sojourner by divine call: "Go from your country and your kindred and your father's house to the land that I will show you" (Gen. 12:1, RSV). "Here already is the obvious, the poignancy of a permanent departure from home. Like three heavy blows are the phrases about country, kindred, and house. Even more moving is the mysterious uncertainty about their destination. The author of Hebrews understood this as he recalled the long story of the fathers, how Abraham went, not knowing where he was to go (Heb. 11:8). This would be the recurring theme of refugee wandering through the centuries."[23] Other patriarchs became sojourners. Isaac, after having gone to Abimelech, in Gerar was a sojourner who sought protection from the Philistines (Gen. 26:1-11). Jacob sojourned with Laban (31:3-7). Esau sojourned in Canaan, increased his wealth and flocks and moved to Seir (36:6-8). The promise to Abraham (17:7-8), that God would give to Abraham's descendants the land of Canaan, the land in which they dwelt as sojourners (Ps. 105:6-15; 1 Chron. 16:13-33), was reiterated in Isaac's blessing upon Jacob (Gen.

28:1-4). The promise was further disclosed to Moses (Ex. 6:4). Pharaoh asked Joseph's brothers to dwell in the land of Goshen and oversee his cattle (Gen. 47:1-6). Israel sojourned in Egypt (Isa. 52:4) and was oppressed (Gen. 15:13; Deut. 26:5-11; Ps. 105:23-35; Acts 7:6). As a sojourner, David made his own the interests of his Philistine patron, Achish (1 Sam. 27:2-3; 12; 28:1ff).

Throughout the Old Testament there are various reasons why the people of God became sojourners:

1. To escape famine (Ruth 1:1; 2 Kings 8:1).
2. To escape military attack (2 Sam. 4:3).
3. To find sanctuary after the destruction of their land by conquest (Isa. 16:4).
4. To participate in the celebration of the Feast of Weeks (Ex. 34:22).
5. To maintain a nomadic ideal (Jer. 35:7).
6. To find a place where they could perform their function, as was the case of the Levites (Judg. 17–18; 19:1; Deut. 12:12; 16:11).

Laws were later established to provide for the stranger and the sojourner. Those who sojourned enjoyed certain privileges. They were not to be oppressed (Ex. 22:21). They were permitted to glean the vineyard and harvest for food provisions (Lev. 19:10; 23:22; Deut. 24:19-21). The cities of refuge provided protection (Num. 35:15; Josh. 20:9). Although most were poor, some apparently became wealthy (Lev. 25:47ff; Deut. 28:43).

All who sojourned in their midst were encouraged to participate in the religious life of the nation. Some observed the sabbath as a day of rest (Ex. 20:10; 23:12), rejoiced in the Feast of Tabernacles (Deut. 16), observed the Day of Atonement (Lev. 16:29-34), and "had no leavened bread on the Feast of Unleavened Bread" (Ex. 12:19).

The New Testament often refers to those truths of faith,

especially Paul's Epistle to the Hebrews. The sojourner, stranger, exile, or refugee may "become through Christ a full member of the household of God."[24] (Also see Eph. 2:11-19). The people of God are to receive strangers hospitably "for thereby some have entertained angels unawares" (Heb. 13:2).

The modern-day sojourner flees to escape famine, destruction, and oppression. The sojourner comes to the United States, seeking to become "a person who occupies a position between that of a native born and the foreigner. The sojourner becomes a person whose status and privileges derive from the bond of hospitality in which the guest is inviolable."[25]

Modern-day sojourners come to the United States seeking a new life. The people of God, the church, should recall the words of Jesus, "I was a stranger, and ye took me in" (Matt. 25:35), and seek to welcome and assist these fellow pilgrims and refugees who come in search of the city which is to come with foundations of love and justice, whose architect and builder is God (see Heb. 11:10).

Nguyen Vu Tran Nguyen was one of seventeen children from around the world chosen to receive the 1984 International Children's Peace Prize. The fifth-grade student at Newton Estates Elementary School wrote an essay about his past in war-torn Vietnam and his new life in Atlanta, Georgia.

Nguyen represented the United States on June 1, 1984, in San Francisco where Mrs. Anwar Sadat and Nobel Peace Prize winner Linus Pauling presented the awards. Nguyen and his family are active members of the Vietnamese congregation of Second Ponce de Leon Baptist Church in Atlanta.

Boualom Inthathirath and her husband were elementary school teachers in Laos for ten years. Communists occupying their country regarded those who worked for the Laotian government as enemies.

They walked all night to the border with Thailand, giving medicine to their three-year-old daughter several times to make her sleep and keep her quiet during the escape trip.

They crossed the Mekong River, the border, into Thailand by boat. In Thailand, they were jailed for a month for entering the country without permission. Then they were sent to a refugee camp where more than twenty thousand people lived. After a year in the camp, the family was resettled in Little Rock, Arkansas.

Boualom, a Buddhist, heard about a Christian who drove people to church. The man and his wife worked hard to help Boualom and other refugees. They often gave time to take someone to the hospital, to find a job, to ask assistance at Social Security offices, or to get a driver's license. As a result of their concern, Boualom became a Christian.

Refugee resettlement has given Southern Baptists an unusual opportunity in ethnic church planting. Persons seeking to resettle in the United States are processed by the Southern Baptist Refugee Resettlement Office in cooperation with the state conventions, local associations, and local churches. The local church approach has proven to be most effective in providing an opportunity to witness through action, deed, and word. Initiated during the Indochinese crisis, the program currently focuses on refugees from throughout the world.

A recent study indicates that the sponsor churches provided 361 ministries encompassing sixteen various types, such as English as a second language (ESL), help to secure employment, et cetera. The outreach to these new Americans has resulted in 47,586 who attend one of the 649 congregations established; that is forty new churches a year for sixteen years.

The world is coming to America; America is a mission field.

Contextual Language Materials

The Bible is the basic document that serves as the proclaimer of the gospel message. The development of literature for evangelism, church development, and missions is essential to the spiritual maturity of the people and the growth of the church.

Baptists have historically published language materials for use on the foreign mission field. These materials were graciously made available to the language-culture churches in America. My experience as a missionary and pastor led to the realization that, although these are excellent materials, their focus is to the foreign mission field in terminology, program, cultural context, psychology, philosophy of life, and especially in the congregations' relationships to a national (foreign) convention.

Ethnic groups in America are not only diverse, but they live in changing cultural and linguistic patterns. Each group continually influences others. Wisdom called for the development of contextual language materials designed for America's diverse mission field. These materials must contain the program emphasis of the Southern Baptist Convention, thus encouraging the ethnic diversity to unify in the life of the denomination.

Seeking to involve the Hispanic churches in the life of the denomination, the Home Mission Board, under the leadership of Dr. Loyd Corder in the early 1950s, began to publish *Nuestra Tarea* (Our Task), a missions education periodical, in cooperation with Woman's Missionary Union. The first Spanish-language stewardship materials were written by Isaac V. Pérez, whose responsibility was to lead Hispanic churches in Texas in stewardship growth. Both of these endeavors proved successful as the contribution to world missions through the Cooperative Program increased each year. It is estimated that Hispanic churches throughout the nation currently contribute in excess of $1.5 million to mission causes annually.

In 1957 the Language Missions Leadership Conference participants began to explore the publication of contextual language materials by the Baptist Sunday School Board. Within a decade representatives from the Baptist Sunday School Board, Woman's Missionary Union, Brotherhood Commission, and Stewardship Commission began to meet to discuss the needs and feasibility for the publication of contextual language materials. These agencies were joined by the Annuity Board in the late 1960s, thus forming the Contextual Language Materials Consortium. The desire for the publication of the needed materials resulted in the WMU, Sunday School Board, and Brotherhood Commission establishing units within their organization whose task is to develop, publish, and field service contextual language materials. In 1978 the Foreign Mission Board began to send a representative to the Consortium meetings.

Although the Consortium existed informally and was working effectively, the executives of the Foreign Mission Board, Home Mission Board, and Sunday School Board suggested the preparation of a formal document in 1990. The other agencies concurred with the purpose and also agreed to work cooperatively.

The Consortium, a partnership of the participating entities, has proven effective beyond expectations. The priority criteria are: (1) what is needed; (2) is it available; (3) is it relevant/ adaptable; (4) should it be published; (5) will the responsible program produce the needed material; and (6) who can produce the needed material? The entity responsible for the publication of the material is also responsible for the promotion, sale, and field servicing.

The Language Church Extension Division, HMB, produces a catalog that contains a listing of the contextual language materials produced for use by ethnic Southern Baptists. Today contextual language materials, for use on the mission field in America, are produced in sixteen languages by eight of the agencies. The quality and content of the various periodicals and materials is such that these are used among ethnic groups in other nations.

The lack of contextually relevant language-culture materials for Southern Baptist churches in the United States is a

Conventionwide problem. Churches, associations, and state conventions also share an interest in having such materials. For this reason, the needs of the local churches, associations, and state conventions are integral parts of the Consortium.

Diversity is a trend which is shaping our lives. As John Naisbitt has written, "We have moved from the myth of the melting pot to a celebration of cultural diversity."[26] This celebration of cultural diversity has touched Southern Baptist life. Within the fifty states, Puerto Rico, and American Samoa, Southern Baptists study the Bible and worship in 102 languages and dialects.

By coordinating existing resources to meet this need, the Southern Baptist Convention demonstrates wise stewardship of human and financial resources. More importantly, the SBC will accelerate the process of reaching ethnics and developing language-culture congregations in this nation.

Field Experiences

1. A Catalog of Contextual Language Materials has been compiled to assist churches in locating available materials for use in the United States.
2. State convention staffs prepare materials and field service the various programs.
3. Eight of the SBC agencies currently produce Contextual Language Materials for use in America's mission field. These are Woman's Missionary Union, Brotherhood Commission, Baptist Sunday School Board, Annuity Board, Home Mission Board, Foreign Mission Board, Stewardship Commission, and Christian Life Commission.
   The first six agencies have staff personnel whose responsibility is to publish contextual language materials for use by Southern Baptists in the United States.

Equipping for Church Growth

Jesus set the example of giving careful attention to the training of men who would do His work. From among those who were called His disciples, He chose twelve that He named apostles (Luke 6:13-16). From the twelve, he chose three for special attention. Peter, James, and John were privileged to be invited into the sick room of Jarius's daughter (Mark 5:37); they alone got to go up to the mount of transfiguration (9:2); and during the agony at Gethsemane they were the closest while He prayed (14:33). Of these three, John was known as "the disciple whom Jesus loved" (John 21:20). These and other Scriptures in the New Testament make it plain that Jesus concentrated His efforts upon comparatively few people in order to train them to impact the world, which was the object of His love.

The relationship of Paul and Timothy is commonly known. Paul took special care in training Timothy and called him his dear son (2 Tim. 1:2). Timothy was not the only one Paul trained one-on-one. Paul wrote in 2 Corinthians 2:12-13 that, when he came to Troas to preach Christ's gospel, he found an open door, but could not rest because his brother, Titus, was not there. Paul turned down the opportunity to preach to the whole of Troas and left to search for Titus. Why? Paul believed that by training Titus he would double the effectiveness of his ministry, and together they could reach two cities like Troas.

Paul learned to do this from Barnabas. When Paul was a new Christian and everyone was afraid of him, it was Barnabas who took hold of Paul and "brought him to the apostles" (Acts 9:27). When a revival broke out in Antioch, Barnabas saw the challenge and left for Tarsus to hunt for Paul. When he found Paul, Barnabas brought him back to Antioch where Paul helped him train new converts for two years. Paul learned much from Barnabas in those two years (11:19-26).

There was such a relationship between Paul and John Mark, also (Acts 13:13; 2 Tim. 4:11). History records that John discipled Polycarp who discipled Irenaeus. Mentorship has its genesis in the New Testament. This should be no surprise since the Hebrew method of training young men was to apprentice them to skilled workers.

Experience and studies indicate that church planting and development are in proportion to the availability of leaders from among the people. Southern Baptists' ability to equip leaders with cultural and linguistic qualities that prepare them to serve in multiple, contextual settings will, to a great extent, determine "the nature and effectiveness of their mission in the year(s) ahead."[35]

The design calls for equipping to a theological base, an understanding of Baptist history, polity, evangelism, and missions. These and other disciplines, such as the cultural aspects of the particular ethnic group, serve as cohesive factors leading to participatory involvement in the denomination. These will equip leaders:

1. Ethnic Leadership Development (ELD) centers—programs in languages other than English, taught in off-campus centers for earning Certificate in Christian Ministry, Diploma in Theology/Religious Education/Music, and Associate of Divinity.
2. Curriculum enrichment—infusing ethnic church growth concepts, information, programs, et cetera, into existing courses, especially evangelism, missions, and history.
3. Language Missions courses—including Language Missions courses in the curriculum of the respective institution.
4. Modern language courses—teaching modern language(s) to help future pastors/leaders (Anglo and ethnic) to minister in changing cultural patterns.
5. Degree exchange/upgrade—developing a curriculum for persons who acquire a theological education in other parts of the world to participate in selected disciplines in

order to become knowledgeable in Southern Baptist history, polity, denominational programs, and so forth.

6. Graduate programs—developing an ethnic track in the Doctor of Ministry and the Doctor of Philosophy programs.

7. Continuing Education—developing seminars and conferences in conjunction with various entities for which Continuing Education Units (CEUs) are granted.

The Ethnic Leadership Development concept (ELD) has proven to be a viable, practical, inexpensive, and successful program. Currently there are 105 centers located throughout the nation, in the urban areas, reservations, villages, et cetera. These centers equip more than fifteen-hundred leaders from among fifteen ethnic groups in twelve languages in addition to American English. These centers use a plan of study that is acceptable to the institution issuing the recognition certificate; yet they are operated locally and are basically supported from the tuition paid by those seeking to prepare themselves to be a better servant of the Lord.

A review of the Navajo work in the 1960s indicated that the twenty-five congregations were all served by "appointed missionaries" and the buildings were built by someone else. The missions work was highly subsidized. In 1965 a conference was held in Gallup, New Mexico, with a focus on the training of leaders for the development of indigenous churches.

Ten years later, there were fifty-eight congregations, with most of these served by Navajo pastors. The congregations met in "hogans" rather than in southern-style church buildings. The Begaye brothers, Russell and Andrew, are among the leaders that emerged from these people. Andrew is a catalytic missionary on the reservation. Russell is on the staff of the Home Mission Board providing leadership among the 475 Native American churches affiliated with the Southern Baptist Convention.

Schools of Prophets

Messengers of the Word, secularly employed pastors and lay leaders, are essential to the task of evangelizing ethnic America. Schools of Prophets, three to six days in length, are designed to improve their skills in order to minister effectively.

The Schools of Prophets basic purpose calls for designing an equipping program to meet the contextual needs of the target group. Its objectives are:

1. To equip ethnic leaders with appropriate ministry skills.
2. To orient ethnic leaders to Southern Baptist denominational life, programs, polity, and practice.
3. To provide intensive biblical training to ethnic leaders within their ethnolinguistic context.
4. To recognize and certify participants' acquisition of skills.

The equipping opportunities are held by regions. These vary in length, from three to six days. The participants earn Continuing Education Units. Upon completion of the training program, participants will be presented a certificate.

The first School of Prophets, held in Tennessee, was attended by 300 people. Since it was held on a weekend, entire families attended. Arrangements had been made for conferences and activities that provided learning experiences for everyone. Special conferences were held for pastors and other church leaders. The evening sessions were of a worship and evangelistic nature. Several people accepted Christ as their Lord and others rededicated their lives.

In 1990 there were twenty-three Schools of Prophets with an enrollment of more than fifteen-hundred people, representing eleven ethnic groups. There were thirty-two professions of faith, seven surrendered for the ministry, and seventy-five pastors were equipped for service. The groups represented 187 churches. The cost of the school was the responsibility of those who attended.

Kairos—Act Now

Kairos is a mentorship approach to equip selected persons as future leaders in ethnic missions. There are two phases to the program. One is the field experience in an urban area. The participant has the opportunity to achieve five goals: (1) to verify the ethnicity; (2) to initiate new work; (3) to enlist and equip leaders; (4) to strengthen existing congregations; and (5) to design a long-range strategy. These goals can be achieved by using the concepts of Laser Thrust, Catalytic Missions, Kaleidoscopic Church Growth, and Microcosmic Urban Strategy.

The second phase of the program is academic. The program is related to a cooperating institution of higher learning which provides the academic components. Upon completion of the program the participant could be eligible for earning a Masters degree in Ethnic Missions.

Ethnic Fellowships

"The genesis of Baptist cooperative bodies is found in the conference in Jerusalem (Acts 15; Gal. 2) and in the cooperative benevolence of New Testament churches (Acts 11:27-30; 2 Cor. 8–9; Rom. 15:15-32; 1 Cor. 16:2-6)."[28] Each church was independent and autonomous, but sympathetic in its understanding and cooperative effort. They were interdependent. The church in Jerusalem had no control over the church in Antioch; yet it was interested in the young church (Acts 11:22). There was a mutual spirit of concern (vv. 29-30).

Church

The local church is the first and oldest unit of Baptist life. The church is a local democratic assembly. Its membership is regenerated. It is autonomous in its operation and has the responsibility to proclaim the gospel. The church seeks to share the gospel with all persons.

"The local church, in cooperation with other local churches, unites its efforts and resources to share the gospel in accordance with the mandate of Christ."[29] "The second unit is the association."[30]

Association

Baptist associations have existed for almost two hundred years. As early as 1642-43, Baptist associations were convening among English Baptists for counsel and correspondence. By 1655 several groups had been formed; and the title "association" was well recognized.[31] The Philadelphia Association was organized in 1707. The organization formed "an association of messengers authorized by their respective churches to mediate and execute designs of public good."[32] This plan was similar to that of associations in England and Wales. In defining its relation to the churches, the plan established the patterns for Baptist associations of the future. "The association had no authority over the churches except as fellowship might be withdrawn from churches for defections in doctrine and practice."[33] The Charleston association, organized in 1751, was the first in the South.

American Indian associations existed in 1842, three years before the organization of the Southern Baptist Convention.

"The average Southern Baptist conceives the association of Baptist churches with which it is affiliated to be an organization through which it voluntarily cooperates with other member churches for special missions ministries within the associational areas, and from which it gains the values such as organization can contribute to the churches in the manifold areas of interest and cooperation."[34] The association is free to determine what churches it will admit into its fellowship and whether or not it will continue to receive the messengers of those who have already been admitted. The churches, also, are free to decide whether or not they will continue to be in a cooperative relationship with the association. The late E. P. Allredge, in the *Southern Baptist Handbook,* gave in essence the following statement as to the function of the association: it exists for "fellowship, conference, and cooperative service."[35]

State

"Baptist cooperation is made necessary by tasks too large for a small number of Christians to accomplish or tasks in which the cooperation of a large number of Christians is more efficient and more effective."[36] This is the theoretical basis for which the state conventions and the Southern Baptist Convention exist. Each is to enable Baptist churches to serve the mission, educational, benevolent, stewardship, civic, fellowship, and many other needs throughout the respective areas and to extend their ministry around the world. Each Baptist entity—local church, association, state convention, and Southern Baptist Convention—is autonomous, yet interdependent in its efforts "to provide mutual aid, Christian fellowship and is designed to encourage Christian growth and to bear a witness to the gospel throughout the world."[37]

National

A review of the various meetings related to the annual meeting of the Southern Baptist Convention indicates that several "fellowship-type" national organizations also meet during this period each year. Some of these are the Pastors Conference, Woman's Missionary Union, Religious Education Association, Music Conference, Southern Baptist Evangelists, Southern Baptist Research Fellowship, and Pastors Wives Fellowship. These are only some of fifteen such organizations active in Southern Baptist life.

A review of the documents which serve as the basis for several of the above fellowships indicate one or more of the following as their objectives: (1) to fellowship, a source of inspiration;[38] (2) to contribute to a better understanding of the church and the denomination;[39] (3) to provide an identity;[40] (4) to provide a competency and assist in acquiring skills;[41] (5)

to serve in an advisory capacity;[42] (6) to serve to effect changes in Southern Baptist agencies;[43] (7) to communicate in a more effective and visible way;[44] (8) to provide an interpretation of trends;[45] (9) to serve in helping to effect changes;[46] (10) to act as a teaching instrument.[47]

The documents sent by five of the organizations responding to an inquiry indicate the following: 1. That dues and/or special offerings are required for membership. 2. That persons with similar interests are welcomed into the membership. 3. That members must be Southern Baptists.

It is common knowledge that several of the other fellowships charge a registration fee, take an offering, and/or include an amount for expenses when meals are served. The following characteristics seem to be associated with those participants in the fellowships: (1) educational attainment; (2) economic and social status; (3) professional competency; (4) special interest; (5) use of "particular" language usage and terminology; (6) similar religious experience; (7) participant in a Southern Baptist program.

In a sense, these are cultural organizations seeking to serve the work of the kingdom. These groups have provided the opportunity for greater expression and participation of interested individuals and for the development of natural leaders. These so-called "special interest groups" have historically contributed to the development of the denomination, as well as served as a source of information as to the needs of Southern Baptist people and churches.

Ethnic Baptist Fellowships

Historically, the Home Mission Board, in keeping with its charter to serve "as a channel... for obedience to Christ's command at home... and to evangelize the savage Indian and the foreigner in our land...," has sought to share the gospel with all people. During the first hundred years, primary attention was given to the American Indians and Spanish in the

Southwest. The 1950s was the beginning of expansion to include other ethnic groups. This effort led to the selection of state and/or area leaders who sought to develop the existing congregations and to establish new work. These leaders created an awareness and an acceptance of ethnic people and congregations as part of Southern Baptist life. People responded positively to the concern of the "Anglo" brethren. Yet because of relations, experience, and language and cultural variances, the ethnic/language-culture churches, even when they have achieved self-support, continue to look to the Home Mission Board for counsel, guidance, interpretation, leadership, and so forth. To many, Language Missions is the Home Mission Board and/or the Southern Baptist Convention.

Historical Overview

Prior to the Civil War, the Choctaw-Creek-Seminole Baptist Association was functioning in Oklahoma Indian territory. Language usage was the dominant reason for the group to organize into two associations—the Choctaw Association and the Creek-Seminole Association. These two associations were in existence prior to the organization of the Oklahoma Baptist Convention, which merged with the Oklahoma Baptist State Convention and became the Baptist General Convention of the State of Oklahoma in 1906. Although the Baptist General Convention of the State of Oklahoma assisted and encouraged the work of the Indian associations, it has been only in the last ten years that these have become an integral part of the state convention.

The Convención Bautista Mexicana de Texas, composed of churches begun under the leadership of the Southern Baptist Convention, was organized in 1910. Language, culture, economics, education, and social acceptance were some of the reasons for its organization. The Convención basically followed the Southern Baptist program and cooperated with the various agencies in its efforts to carry out the Great Commission. The organization of Spanish associations was encouraged across the state, until today there are some twenty such fellowships in Texas. The mid-1950s brought the unification between the Mexican Baptist Convention of Texas and The Baptist General Convention of Texas. In 1964 unification was finalized, thus providing a closer working relationship between Hispanic and Anglo Baptists in Texas.

The Convención Bautista Hispana de Nuevo Mexico has been in existence for more than fifty years. There are three Hispanic associations throughout the state. The Convención, in recent years, has begun to work in cooperation with The Baptist Convention of New Mexico. To the best of my knowledge, it continues to be an autonomous organization with its member churches having a dual affiliation.

The Southern Baptist Conference of the Deaf was organized in 1950. The group meets annually. The Home Mission Board provides counsel and guidance.

Existing Fellowships

Currently there are at least seventy-five ethnic fellowships (associations) composed of Southern Baptist ethnic/language-culture churches. These fellowships, confraternities, associations, conventions, conferences, and camp meetings have come into existence to:

1. Encourage and maintain a spirit of fellowship.
2. Meet the individual needs of churches.
3. Encourage the churches to undergird and participate in programs of the Southern Baptist Convention, including gifts to world missions through the Cooperative Program.
4. Serve as a link with the "Anglo" associations and state conventions, when necessary.

The various meetings are conducted in the language of the people, within their cultural context, in a familiar setting, and at a time convenient for the participation of the people. Often, the attendance at these meetings is greater than the numerical presence at the annual meeting of the "local" association. Such meetings provide the opportunities for development of natural leaders and dialogue, which the language-culture persons would not be given the opportunity to do in most meetings.

Tarrant Baptist Association (Fort Worth, Texas) in the mid-1950s encouraged its Hispanic churches to conduct special Spanish-language meetings for their edification and fellowship. Associational leaders gave guidance to the program content. The associational budget included an amount for such meetings. Thus the Hispanic churches contributed to the association, as well as to the Cooperative Program. This basic approach has been emulated by many associations and state conventions with various approaches. Some characteristics of those participating in the ethnic fellowships are: (1) religious heritage; (2) education; (3) economic and social status; (4) special interest in persons with a unique cultural heritage; (5) language usage; (6) cultural cohesiveness; (7) enthusiastic participation with persons of similar background—identity.

These organizations provide an opportunity for fellowship, expression, interpretation of the denomination, leadership development, creation of an awareness of their needs, and preparation for evangelizing persons of a similar background.

Ethnic fellowships have contributed to the development of ethnic/language-culture churches; thus the Southern Baptist Convention is the most integrated denomination in the nation. The Southern Baptist Convention is, perhaps, the largest Spanish-speaking Baptist convention in the world. The unique ability and polity of the denomination is the key to responsiveness of language-culture persons who do not have to be "Americanized" to become Christians.

State conventions where an ethnic fellowship exists have followed a similar pattern of providing leadership and encouraging contextualized meetings, which develop leaders and undergird Convention programs.

Leadership Role

Language Missions personnel seek to provide leadership, interpret the denomination to the churches, and the churches to the agencies, serve as a liaison and encourage the existing ethnic organizations to support SBC programs and to focus these to meet the needs of this particular segment of Southern Baptist life. The Polish, Hungarian, and Romanian conventions and/or conferences and others are composed of churches that are dually affiliated, many of which are located in Canada and other countries.

Changing ethnic patterns in the nation, the increasing migration, and the concern to evangelize rather than to "Americanize" have resulted in a response of ethnic persons unparalleled in Christian history. The exposure of ethnic/language-culture Southern Baptists to the various aspects and programs of the denomination has brought about an awareness that their needs are not being met and/or will not be met. This, together with the knowledge that God has equipped them with a unique heritage to reach a segment of America that the typical Baptist church and/or organization will never reach, generates a desire to contribute to the missionary endeavor at home and abroad.

In recent years, the Chinese Fellowship of North America, the Korean Southern Baptist Pastors Conference, the Hispanic Southern Baptist Fellowship and the Messianic Baptist Fellowship have emerged in the life of the denomination. The American Indians have also developed their own fellowship. The emerging fellowships have sought and welcomed the counsel of the Language Church Extension Division, but have never requested permission to exercise their privilege as Southern Baptists—to come together to extend the work of the kingdom.

An Approach to Ethnic Fellowships

Southern Baptists are faced with the alternative—to lead or abdicate their leadership of ethnic fellowships which seek to strengthen and expand the work of the denomination. Lyle Schaller has stated that, "to a substantial extent, the growing religious bodies of the next dozen years will be those religious bodies which: (1) affirm the legitimacy of the ethnic church; (2) encourage a bilingual approach to the preaching of the Word; (3) affirm a pluralistic style of church life; (4) are not locked into exclusionary procedures; (5) recognize and accept ethnic congregations; (6) involve the ethnic congregations in the ongoing life of the denomination."[48]

Although there are those who see the ethnic fellowships as divisive, the majority are of the opinion that the Home Mission Board should seek to wisely provide leadership and guidance as the ethnic fellowships emerge "naturally." Such an approach calls for the development of an ethnic liaison subprogram as part of the Program of Language Missions. The following is but a sketch of suggested guidelines in relating to the various ethnic fellowships which are of a regional and/or national scope. These guidelines would in essence be in two sections.

Section One—Ethnic Fellowships

1. To lead churches to actively participate in Southern Baptist life.
2. To encourage the churches to contribute to world missions through the Cooperative Program.
3. To focus Southern Baptist programs to meet the needs of ethnic/language-culture congregations.
4. To see that projects of special interest to the group are in cooperation with Southern Baptist programs and financial plans.

Section Two—Language Church Extension Division

1. To provide denominational leadership.
2. To serve as liaison with the Convention agencies and programs.
3. To interpret the denomination.
4. To undergird to the best of its ability in keeping with the program statement.

These would be implemented in keeping with the objective of the fellowship and within the policies and procedures of the Home Mission Board and the Southern Baptist Convention.

Assertiveness of the 1990s

The ethnic assertiveness of the 1990s is marked by wide-spread pluralism. Sharing the gospel in a pluralistic society, in essence, calls for the development of the contextualized, denominationally-oriented, indigenous concept of the New Testament church. It should be contextualized in that it is woven into the culture of the groups and gradually influences the value system in keeping with biblical teachings. It should be denominationally-oriented in that it becomes an active part of, is accepted by, and contributes to the life of the denomination. In a sense it nourishes as well as receives nourishment from its relationships, one with the other. It should be indigenous in that it supports itself in keeping with the ability of the people, governs itself, and uses its natural and social channels for multiplying the body of Christ. The unique development of such an approach in the life of the denomination calls for dependence upon God for wisdom and leadership and the affirming of our trust in the people of God whom He entrusted with the Great Commission—"Go . . . preach."

Field Experiences

1. The following are national ethnic fellowships: Arabic, American Indian, Cambodian, Chinese, Deaf, Hispanic, Hmong, Hungarian, Italian, Japanese, Korean, Laotian,

Messianic, Polish, Romanian, Russian-Ukrainian, Ukrainian, and Vietnamese.

2. There are twenty-one state fellowships in the various state conventions.

3. There are forty-four area/associational fellowships in the state conventions.

Ethnic congregations are an integral part of Southern Baptist life. The emphasis and programs of the denomination are focused toward the language-culture churches. These congregations use the information, suggestions, and so forth, to develop their own programs.

People from the various congregations are elected to serve as trustees of institutions and on boards and commissions of state and national entities. These people are elected as a part of the normal ongoing process and not on a parity basis. Ethnics serve on the staff of local associations, institutions, state conventions, and national agencies.

The ethnic congregations send messengers (delegates) to represent them in the work of the local association, state convention, and the Southern Baptist Convention. Each congregation has the opportunity to support the mission work by contributing to either the local association or world missions through the Cooperative Program.

Gradually a national strategy is being developed by the fellowships. Thus far, the ethnic leaders have identified over 20,000 places for planting ethnic congregations.

Southern Baptist polity, the centrality of the Bible, the priesthood of the believer, and the autonomy of the local church permit ethnic people to cherish their heritage and be a part of the denomination. In a sense, not only is the gospel woven into the ethnic fabric, but the flexibility of the denomination permits the ethnic churches to be Christian and Southern Baptist without having to negate their cultural and linguistic (contextual) heritage.

The emerging trends among "Anglo" Southern Baptists seem to forecast the emergence of a national federation of Baptists; a federation that permits diversity, yet unity in missions and evangelism.

Methods

Methods, the means of achieving a goal through the systematic arrangement and communication of ideas, topics, et cetera, should be developed in keeping with the particular ethnic group. Because ethnic people in America live in changing cultural patterns, existing methods may be adapted successfully. Southern Baptists have, in many instances, adapted and/or translated rural-oriented methods that have been successful in many instances. However, these methods are gradually becoming obsolete as the nation increasingly becomes an ethnic and urban society.

Methods should be developed in keeping with the societal, economic, educational, and religious context of the particular ethnic group. Pragmatical, current methods should be used to "inject" the gospel with a gradual development of contextual methods. In a sense, "the influence of American pragmatism and the ethnic philosophical view of life must be fused in the development of a methodology which is relevant to the ethnic church in a pluralistic society."

Church Growth Holography

Often it is assumed that all church growth is measured in the same manner. Thus the idea is erroneous that an ethnic church develops and achieves the same growth as an Anglo church whose members have an evangelical background.

Holograms ("whole message" Greek) are three-dimensional images created by exposing an object to enable the viewing of the unforeseeable in order to determine the actual. Church Growth Holography provides a three-dimensional view of the ethnic church—numerical, contextual, and cultural —in order to evaluate the actual growth. The consideration of the contextual and socio-religious factors of an ethnic church are essential for an effective, true evaluation. The gospel must be wrapped in a container that is acceptable to the people. The type and color of the container must attract the "client" to want its contents. Information about the culturally acceptable package must be communicated on the label in the language of the people. The gospel can best be understood and accepted when it is shared within the context of the people.

Notes

1. *International Bulletin of Missionary Research*, (New York: Hochman Associates, October 1981), vol. 5, no. 4, 175.
2. Bruce C. E. Fleming, *Contextualization of Theology*, (Pasadena: William Carey Library, 1980), 7.
3. Ibid., 7.
4. Ibid., 65.
5. Ibid., 64.
6. Ibid., 71.
7. R. Daniel Shaw, *Transculturation*, (Pasadena: William Carey Library, 1988), 19.
8. David J. Hesselgrave and Edward Rommen, *Contextualization*, (Grand Rapids: Baker Book House, 1988), 1.
9. Ibid., 9.
10. Ibid., 30.
11. Ibid., 11.
12. Ibid., 15.
13. Spiros Zodhiates, ed., *The Hebrew-Greek Study Bible, New American Standard*, (La Habra, Calif.: The Lockman Foundation), 1,434.
14. Jaime G. Prieto, *The Development of A Filipino Ministry in Honolulu with the Hawaii Baptist Convention*, (Atlanta: Home Mission Board, 1986), unpublished doctoral thesis, 23.
15. J. S. Excell and H.D.M. Spence, eds., *Commentary on St. Matthew, The Pulpit Commentary*, (Grand Rapids: William B. Eerdmans Publishing Co., 1978), 645.
16. E. C. Pentecost, *Issues in Missiology: An Introduction*, (Grand Rapids: Baker Book House, 1982), 29.
17. *Encyclopedia Britannica*, (Chicago: William Benton Publisher, 1973), vol. 6, 254.

18. Talmadge R. Amberson, *The Birth of Churches,* (Nashville: Broadman Press, 1978), 12.

19. Solomon Dowis, *O Jerusalem, Our Cities for Christ,* (Atlanta: Home Mission Board, 1951).

20. Jack Redford, *Guide For Establishing New Churches,* (Atlanta: Home Mission Board), 5.

21. John F. Kennedy, *A Nation of Immigrants,* (New York: Harper and Row, 1964), 18.

22. Frederick A. Norwood, *Strangers and Exiles,* (Nashville and New York: Abingdon Press, 1969), vol. 1, 4.

23. Ibid., 23.

24. Ephesians 2:11-19; Tenney, 449.

25. Buttrick, vol. 4, 397.

26. John Naisbitt, *Megatrends,* (New York: Warner Books, 1982), 244.

27. William Hull, "Pluralism in the Southern Baptist Convention," *Review and Expositor,* (Louisville: Southern Baptist Theological Seminary, Winter, 1982), vol. 79, no. 1, 135.

28. Norman Wade Cox, ed., *Encyclopedia of Southern Baptists,* (Nashville: Broadman Press, 1958), vol. 1, 87.

29. H.H. Hobbs, *Fundamentals of Our Faith,* (Nashville: Broadman Press, 1960), 125.

30. S.F. Dowis, *Associational Guidebook,* (Nashville: Convention Press, 1959), 1.

31. Cox, vol. 1, 87.

32. Cox, vol. 1, 87.

33. Cox, vol. 1, 87.

34. Cox, vol. 1, 88.

35. Dowis, 7.

36. Cox, vol. 1, 318.

37. Cox, vol. 1, 318.

38. "Organizational Guidelines," Conference of Southern Baptist Evangelists.

39. "Organizational Guidelines," Southern Baptist Research Fellowship, (Atlanta: Research Division, Home Mission Board).

40. "Organizational Guidelines," Association of Southern Baptist Campus Ministers.

41. Association of Southern Baptist Campus Ministers.

42. Association of Southern Baptist Campus Ministers.

43. Association of Southern Baptist Campus Ministers.

44. "Organizational Guidelines," Southern Baptist Associational Directors Conference.

45. "Organizational Guidelines," Southern Baptist Religious Education Association.

46. Southern Baptist Associational Directors Conference.

47. Conference of Southern Baptist Evangelists.

48. Lyle E. Schaller, *Understanding Tomorrow,* (Nashville: Abingdon Press, 1976), 75.

5 Ethnic Church Growth

In the mid 1950s I was asked to consider serving in Central America. The trip called for a layover in Mexico City to visit a friend. During the next few days I visited the campus of the University of Mexico. There were magnificent mosaics on the ends of the multistory buildings which portrayed the history of the nation and its people. The mosaics were made of small pieces, each to fit into a certain area. Each piece was uniquely made by hand by an accomplished artisan, and was glazed to reflect light. The eyes of the various figures seemed to be focused on the individual observer, regardless of where one stood. The mosaic was incomplete if even one piece were missing.

In a sense the United States is a mosaic of people brought together by God in a selected part of the world. It could be said that ours is a global nation. Such was the attraction to the mosaics and the insight they provided that it was evident that the world was in America. Aware that the melting-pot concept was a myth, I began to envision what would happen to the proclamation of the gospel worldwide when Christianity would decline in America. Therefore, if there is to be a witness around the world, then the Scripture, "Ye shall be witnesses unto me both in Jerusalem, . . . Samaria, and unto the uttermost part of the earth" (Acts 1:8), provides the vision for evangelizing the world by reaching the ethnic groups in

America for Christ. I decided while waiting to board the plane from Mexico City to Dallas, to continue to serve among ethnic groups in America. This began a pilgrimage that, unknown to me, would impact ethnic/language-culture missionary endeavors not only in the Southern Baptist Convention, but among other denominations and in numerous countries around the world. In a sense, it was the beginning of the Language Missions Philosophy.

The ethnic assertiveness of the 1960s through the 1990s is marked by widespread pluralism. This calls for the development of approaches which are compatible with the New Testament concept of the church, yet permit the sharing of the gospel contextually. The two approaches, which are interrelated and yet distinct, are Ethnic Church Growth and Transcultural Outreach. These approaches, using the channels for proclamation, language, and culture, provide the framework in the lives of people who comprise a pluralistic society.

Transcultural Outreach

"The transcultural proclamation of the Good News is the sharing from one culture to another the religious experience and concept of God embodied in the scriptures."[1] In a sense, it is the transferring of the concept of God from one culture into another culture. Transcultural Outreach is the effort of an existing homogenous church to share the gospel with persons of another ethnic/language-culture group residing in the community. The use of the concept, Bible study, departments, and so forth, began to emerge in the 1900s when the First Baptist Church in San Antonio, Texas, began Spanish-language Sunday School classes for the Mexican population. These classes were the forerunner of the First Mexican Baptist Church in the city.

The Baptist churches in Miami revived the concept in the 1950s to reach out to the Cuban immigrants who came as a result of the revolution. Today there are over fifty Hispanic churches in that city.

The recent emergence of the "indigenous satellite" approach uses the bases of the concept, encouraging a continual ministry. Transcultural Outreach provides a way for a local church to minister to all the people in the community regardless of culture and language. It also permits the usage of existing facilities initially. Often this has led to the development of a bilingual, bicultural church. In some instances circumstances in which the people live necessitate continuing outreach on the part of the church. However, the people who attend the Transcultural Outreach in their language should themselves determine whether to remain a dependent group or to organize into an autonomous church.

Decades of change in America and the diversity of value systems call for a mission strategy focused on ethnic people. The strategy should consider the nation, especially the urban areas, as a related unit made up of people who live not only in a geographical, professional, and socioeconomical community, but also in the ethnic community. Traditionally, it has been assumed that the ethnic groups have become a part of "America's melting pot." Actually, only a very small percentage have been assimilated. The current polarization taking place throughout the nation shows that these groups resent paternalism, humiliation, and condescension. For too long we have reached down to pull up. It is time that we reached out and embraced with the love of God.

The Ethnic Church

Our pluralistic society calls for an ethnic church. Ethnic Church Growth establishes, nourishes, and multiplies the church in the ethnolinguistic context of the people. Language and culture are channels for communication of the gospel. Language provides the means for expression and participation. Culture provides the cohesive factors that unite people of similar backgrounds, provides fellowship, and determines personal involvement within the group.

The ethnic church, in a sense, becomes a homogeneous unit which in a pluralistic society permits people to help differing human groups live together in greater love and harmony. Yet it permits them the right to be themselves and to worship, witness, and minister in a contextual setting from which emerges a New Testament church.

The development of methods and literature and the equipping of leaders are essential to the development of the ethnic church. Methods, the means of achieving a goal through systematic arrangement of ideas, topics, and so forth should be developed in keeping with the particular ethnic church. These methods should be designed in keeping with the social, economic, educational, and religious background of the specific ethnic group. Use the language of the people: imperative if the goal is to be attained. America's pluralistic context often calls for methods which are biculturally structured, simple to implement, easily understood, and which provide opportunities for fellowship. The influence of American pragmatism and the ethnic philosophical view of life must be fused in the development of a methodology relevant to the ethnic church in a pluralistic society.

Literature in a language other than American English will enhance the development of the ethnic church. Often, such materials should be bilingual. Consideration should be given to the historical, cultural, religious heritage, and the language of the specific group for whom these are prepared. Design and color coordination should be attractive to the group for whom they are intended. The content should seek to present the biblical teachings as they relate to the particular ethnic group. The usage and distribution of these materials will largely depend upon the economic ability of the people.

Growth of the ethnic church is greatly determined by its leaders. Leaders from among the people should be culturally and linguistically compatible with the group they serve. The equipping of these leaders should include the best theological training, without leading them to negate their unique cultural and linguistic abilities. Every effort must be made to encourage leaders from among our various subcultures to commit themselves to the ministry.

The ethnic church will develop in keeping with its concept of time, space, sequence, elements of order, customs, styles, expressions, and emphasis. Its cultural uniqueness and language provide cohesiveness as well as channels for the group to communicate the gospel to others with similar characteristics.

It is imperative that the denomination continually seek to lead the ethnic church to be an active and viable participant. The uniqueness of the ethnic church will enlarge the missionary "vision" of the denomination. It will also provide the denomination with the unique abilities of the ethnic church to carry out the Great Commission.

The ethnic group should be given the opportunity to determine the type of programs it prefers. This will encourage participation and involvement in the life of the church. It is important that the leaders of the church are culturally sensitive and personally related to the ethnic group. Most ethnic groups belong to a face-to-face society and greatly value personal relationships. Such a relationship will enhance the growth and development of the ethnic group as it seeks to understand, live, and practice the concept of God within its own culture. The ethnic group should be consulted as to its needs, plans, participation, et cetera. If possible, these should be incorporated into the ministry focused at the group. Flexibility is essential to a successful ministry.

The existence of various ethnic cultures that make up the "American culture" is the basis for the development of the ethnic church. The integrity of the distinctive cultures and "the right to be different" of the individuals who want to maintain them can and should be respected. This means that "mainline" Americans, especially Southern Baptists, must be careful about regarding as deficiencies certain ethnic traits which may be, from another point of view, desirable characteristics. There must be opportunity for cultural integration without assimilation. However, the establishment should not force values and behavior patterns on any ethnic group. The ethnic church's objective is to bring people of ethnic origin into a right relationship with Jesus Christ.

Ethnic Church Planting

The ethnic church can be defined as planting the gospel seed in a cultural and, perhaps, linguistic context and involving ethnic people in the nurture of this seed within the framework of their needs and abilities. Its natural growth leads it to plan to meet the needs of people, govern its own affairs, multiply itself through ministry and witness, and participate in the evangelization of the world.

Ethnic Church Planting Guide

An Ethnic Church Planting Guide in four phases is suggested for those desiring to penetrate America's mosaic with the gospel of Jesus Christ.

Phase I

1. **Prayer**—The leadership of the Holy Spirit is imperative in ethnic church planting. People committing themselves should seek the empowering of the Spirit as they launch themselves into planting a new congregation in a complex cultural context.
2. **Envision the opportunity**—People are important. The cultural myopic scales need to be shed for a new vision, that all people are important before God. Personal relationships and attitudes need to be examined; and where these are not in tune with God, they should be changed. A visit to the nearby mall or shopping center will help to discern if language-culture people live in an area.

3. **Focus on the people**—People are important. Become acquainted with them. Treat them with kindness and courtesy. Respect them. Accept them as fellow Americans; after all, we are all immigrants or descendants of immigrants.

   Seek to identify the ethnic group(s). Some ethnics are identifiable by their features; others are not. Become their friend. Smile. Offer assistance, such as opening a door, helping to carry an item, et cetera. Be especially respectful of the elderly. Be helpful to the children. If ethnics are your neighbors, be neighborly.

4. **Explore the possibilities**—An outreach among language-culture people is needed in most communities, whether urban or rural. The Laser Thrust has been designed to assist churches in their efforts to share the gospel of Jesus Christ. The *Laser Thrust Guide* is a valuable instrument in exploring the possibilities. It also helps to notice these in your community: Ethnic restaurants, businesses, churches, clubs, and organizations; theaters that show non-English language movies; language (other than English) periodicals; ethnic names in the local telephone directory; ethnic concentrations; people around you who seem to be different. For other ideas, think *What and where do people gather when they don't have anything to do?*

   It is important to avoid being overly inquisitive. Although people generally appreciate our interest, do not be pushy; be yourself. Ethnics are usually cautious when asked about their families and background. Be a friend, not a nuisance.

5. **Segment the people**—Preparation for the Laser Thrust calls for the gathering of data. In a sense, identification or segmentation of the various ethnic groups takes place. The Laser Thrust will help to verify the ethnicity of the area. Segment the ethnic groups, evaluate the

responsiveness of the people to the gospel, discover natural leaders, determine the strength of the existing churches, and help to initiate new work. The information and experience acquired during the Laser Thrust can serve as the basis for the development of a language church planting strategy.

Should it not be feasible to conduct a Laser Thrust, the following inquiries should be made.

Sources of information: Census data, school records, ethnic, social, fraternal, and business organizations, local government offices, regional planning commissioners, charity organizations, language media—newspaper, radio, and television.

Conduct a religious survey.

6. **Establish priorities**—The establishment of priorities can become highly technical and complicated. Keep it simple. Determine the responsiveness to the gospel; are there any "believers" among the people? What is the attitude of the people toward God? Are there any "believers" among the natural leaders? Were the people friendly or just courteous? Did anyone offer their home for a gathering? Did the youth seem responsive, et cetera?

   Begin with the ethnic group that seems responsive and cooperative.

7. **Select the location**—Location selection is very important. There are some groups who will not enter a "Protestant/Baptist" building. Often families will not venture outside of their "world." This is especially true of women. Permission may be granted to meet in a home. Experience indicates that facilities near and accessible to the people are preferable. Do not take children in your car outside of their community without the consent of the family and permission of the man of the house.

8. **Secure the sponsor**—Sponsorship is somewhat similar

to adoption. It is a sacred trust, accepted by those committed to exercise responsible guidance to the new group of New Testament believers. The sponsor provides nourishment and leadership, but is not dictatorial, and guides without "smothering" the adopted congregation (child) entrusted to them by God.

The sponsor will want a committee composed of people from both congregations. The financial investment by the sponsor is known to the congregation. The congregation is led to assume financial responsibility through the handling of its financial operation and gifts to associational missions and world missions through the Cooperative Program.

The sponsor should lead the congregation to develop programs of Bible study, equipping, youth missions education, stewardship, and missions. In addition, such plans should include helping the congregation to acquire its own facilities. Wisdom calls for development of a budget that is within the economic abilities of the people, thus enhancing the congregation to achieve self support.

It is important that the sponsor church not assume a paternalistic, condescending attitude. Remember, God has given the sponsor the responsibility to "rear" this group of believers in Christian maturity and responsibility.

9. **Determine the approaches**—The gospel seed is sown in various contexts; by the road, on the rocky ground, among thorns, and in good soil (Mark 4:3-8). It is rejected, tolerated, ignored, or accepted. The context of each ethnic group varies according to the context of the people—historical, cultural, linguistic, economic, educational, and socioreligious background of the people.

The numerous ethnic groups who are a part of the American mosaic call for two distinct, yet comparable approaches: Ethnic Church Starting and Transcultural Outreach.

Ethnic Church Starting

The linguistic and cultural uniqueness of the people provide the channels for ethnic church planting. The church should worship in a manner that is acceptable and comfortable to the people. The church should have a Bible study program. Other programs featured should be the equipping of leaders, missions education, stewardship, youth activities, mission giving, both local (associational) and worldwide (Cooperative Program).

Facilities used initially may be borrowed or loaned facilities; however, plans should be initiated for acquiring their own buildings. If the sponsor provides the facilities, the church will want to develop a plan for the congregation to own the facilities.

The congregation, beginning with its first meeting, should give those in attendance an opportunity to contribute financially toward the expenses related to their gathering. A budget, within the economic abilities of the people, should be prepared and approved by the group. A treasurer should be selected and held accountable for the use of funds.

In the event the congregation receives financial assistance for its operation, the church should adopt a plan for self-support to be achieved.

Transcultural Outreach

The transcultural proclamation of the good news is the transferring from one culture to another the religious experience and concept of God embodied in the Scriptures.[2] Therefore, Transcultural Outreach becomes the efforts of an existing homogeneous church to share the gospel with people of another ethnic/language-culture group which resides in the community where the church is located.

These efforts by the church may be one or a combination of the following:

1. Be a witness to ethnic/language-culture people in the community.
2. Befriend an ethnic family. Seek to involve them in social events, sports, church activities, as well as invite them to your home.
3. Sponsor a refugee(s). The church sponsors a refugee family and assists them in understanding the "American way of life."
4. Provide a Bible study. Secure Scriptures in the language of the people. Enlist and/or equip someone to lead the group. Sometimes the group may want to study in English, using language Bibles to help them understand.
5. Home fellowships for Bible study could be started. Many who would not come to the "church building" will participate in a Bible study when held in a neighbor's home.
6. Literacy classes may be offered. These may be English classes, or, in some cases, members of the group may want to learn their native language or have their children taught the language.
7. A Sunday School class or department may be provided in the language of the group.
8. A staff member, preferably an associate pastor, who is capable of communicating in the language of the group, should be enlisted.
9. A language radio ministry might be provided to help the people keep abreast of news, become aware of the "American way of life," and share the message of the love of God.[3]

Communication of the gospel can best be effective by observing these principles:

1. Seek to establish a genuine friendship.
2. Recognize the cultural uniqueness.
3. Adapt to the cultural values of the other person.
4. Remember that it is a task of reconciliation.

5. Seek to understand similarities as well as dissimilarities in order to build cultural bridges.
6. Establish true communication; if possible, use the language of the people.
7. Seek to rewrap the gospel in terms of the new culture.

Phase II

1. **Gather the people**—Having considered and utilized the various factors in phase I, plans should be developed to gather the people. This may be done through visitation, phone calls, mail, or the use of mass media. It would be wise to select the leader, whether it is a layperson or a pastor, prior to the announcement for the gathering. Plans should be made to welcome the people. Be prepared for the presence of the entire family. Remember, these people may have never attended an evangelical service. Be kind, courteous, and friendly. Be willing to tolerate people entering and leaving during the service, children crying, and so forth.

2. **Initiate the meeting**—Lead the people to participate in singing and other group activities. This may be the first time many of the people have attended an evangelical/ Protestant worship service. Initiate and maintain a worshipful atmosphere throughout the gathering.

3. **Develop the congregation**—Programs of Bible study, leadership training, stewardship, missions education, music, and so forth, will contribute to the growth of the congregation. These programs should be developed within the context of the people.

   The sponsor church should plan with the congregation toward the organization of the group into a church. The congregation should plan to organize into a self-supporting church.

Phase III

1. **Organize the church**—The sponsor church should plan for the day when its adopted child (mission congregation) is organized into a church. The new church should be in keeping with the laws of the area where the church is located. A constitution, describing the various operational aspects of the new church, should be prepared and agreed upon by the vote of the congregation. The organization includes the adoption of the articles of faith, the church covenant, and other such documents.
2. **Call a leader**—The church should call a pastor who shall lead them spiritually, doctrinally, and so forth. The pastor is responsible to the people for the progress and growth of the church.
3. **Develop the church**—The new church should develop its own plans for growth. A budget within the economic ability of the church should be developed and approved by the vote of the church.

   Plans for acquiring their own facilities should be developed as a part of the constituting of the church. The sponsor church may want to provide a grant or deed the property the congregation has been using. It may be that the church will need to secure a loan in order to own their own property. The ownership should be legal and responsible.

   The new church may need financial assistance to meet its obligations. If such is the case, then plans to achieve self-support should be made when the request is made or soon thereafter.

Phase IV

1. **Partnership**—Partnership comes with the new relationship between the sponsor church and the new church. Each exists to meet specific and unique needs. Both

should pray for and visit each other. This includes helping each other, even financially.

2. **Responsibility**—Responsibility never ceases. It only
   varies in its scope. Families may be segmented; yet they
   continue a relationship of equals as members of the family of God.

The ethnic group should be given the opportunity to determine the type of program it prefers. This will encourage participation and involvement in the life of the church. It is important
that the leaders of the church be culturally sensitive and personally related to the ethnic group. Most ethnic groups belong
to a face-to-face society and greatly value personal relationships. Such relationships will enhance the growth and development of the ethnic group as it seeks to understand, live, and
practice the concept of God within its own culture. The ethnic
group should be consulted as to its needs, plans, participation,
et cetera. If possible, these should be incorporated into the
ministry focused at the group. Flexibility is essential to a successful ministry.

It is imperative that the denomination continually seek to
lead the ethnic church to be an active and viable participant.
The uniqueness of the ethnic church will enlarge the missionary "vision" of the denomination. It will also provide the
denomination with the unique abilities of the ethnic church to
carry out the Great Commission.

Thus it becomes imperative that an effective use of the
channels of communication, language, and culture, among the
various ethnic communities of the nation be utilized to share
the love of God through Jesus Christ. If people are to comprehend the significance of a faith relationship with Jesus Christ, it
is imperative to acknowledge that "faith cometh by hearing,
and hearing by the word of God" (Rom. 10:17). Thus language and culture are the channels for proclamation of the
gospel (Acts 2:5-11).

Sharing the gospel in a pluralistic society in essence calls for the development of the contextualized/denominational/indigenous church. It should be contextualized in that the gospel is woven into the culture of the group and gradually influences the value system in keeping with biblical teachings. It should be denominational in that it becomes an active part of, is accepted by, and contributes to the life of the denomination. In a sense, it nourishes as well as receives nourishment from its relationships, one with the other. It should be indigenous in that it supports itself in keeping with the ability of the people, governs itself in keeping with the structures of the particular group, and uses its natural and social channels for multiplying the body of Christ.

Lyle E. Schaller, in his *Understanding Tomorrow,* states that "to a substantial extent the growing religious bodies of the next dozen years will be those religious bodies which:

1. Affirm the legitimacy of the ethnic church.
2. Encourage a bilingual approach to preaching the Word.
3. Are able to affirm a pluralistic style of church life.
4. Are not locked in to exclusionary procedures in the recognition and acceptance of ethnic congregations.
5. Involve the laity in the ongoing life of the denominational family."

Ethnic Church Development

Once the gospel seed has been planted and results are harvested, attention must be given to the function, nourishment, and multiplication of the ethnic church. This, too, is ethnic church growth and may be referred to as ethnic church development.

The community of believers known as the ethnic church, in all probability, had never known of the existence of the Bible, attended a Christian church, or had any idea how to operate the church.

Edification

The New Testament shares some of the first century church's experiences that can contribute to the growth of the ethnic church. These were experiences that provided the group with opportunities to learn, relate, pray, sing, give, eat, and witness.

The Lord exhorted the believers to teach (Matt. 28:19). The new Christians in Jerusalem "continued steadfastly in the apostles' doctrine" (Acts 2:42). Peter indicates that the new believers were to "As newborn babes, desire the sincere milk of the word, that ye may grow thereby" (1 Pet. 2:2). The ethnic must give serious and continual attention to the teaching of the Scriptures in the language of the people. Methodology may vary and must be effective. These methods should be compatible with the particular ethnic group of the church.

Fellowship

The new believers in Jerusalem continued in "fellowship *[koinonia]* and in breaking of bread, and in prayers" (Acts 2:42). Fellowship is a time of joy, friendship, et cetera, that binds ethnic groups. It is an opportunity to fellowship with others who have experienced a new relationship with Jesus Christ and each other, and to pray for one another, as well as worship God in praise and thanksgiving. The apostle John recognized the importance of fellowship when he wrote, "That which we have seen and heard declare we unto you, that ye also may have fellowship with us: and truly our fellowship is with the Father, and with his Son Jesus Christ" (1 John 1:3). Fellowship unites the family of God on earth.

Prayer

The upper room prayer experience created a spirit of unity and oneness. Nearly 120 believers continually devoted themselves to prayer (Acts 1:15). The Epistles instructed the church to engage in prayer. Paul told the Christians in Rome and

Colossae to devote themselves to prayer (Rom. 12:12; Col. 4:2). The Ephesians and Thessalonians were exhorted to pray at all times and without ceasing (Eph. 6:18; 1 Thess. 5:17). Paul wrote to the Philippians, "Be careful for nothing, but in everything by prayer and supplication with thanksgiving let your requests be made known unto God" (Phil. 4:6). James admonished believers to "pray for one another" (Jas. 5:16). Prayer kept the believers tuned into God's leadership.

Music

The people of God have always enjoyed music. The Old Testament mentions various types of musical expression, especially singing. The disciples, after having eaten the last supper and just before "they went out into the mount of Olives," sang a hymn (Mark 14:26). Paul described singing as "Speaking to yourselves in psalms and hymns and spiritual songs, singing and making melody in your heart to the Lord" (Eph. 5:19).

Giving

Those who were part of the church cared about others. Paul added, "Let us do good unto all men, especially unto them who are of the household of faith (Gal. 6:10; see 1 Thess. 5). Paul believed and thought giving was an essential experience for all believers; "Being enriched in everything to all bountifulness" (2 Cor. 9:11). Christian giving is an outward expression of love.

Evangelism

Another dimension to the edification process is the opportunity for witnessing. The church has to be careful lest it become inward oriented, rather than outward oriented toward proclaiming biblical truths. Acts and the Epistles record the impact made by the first century on the world of that day. Francis A. Schaeffer, in *The Church at the End of the Twentieth Century,*

states that history reports "that in the Greek and Roman world
the cry went out, *behold, how they love one another.*"

Multiplication

The Book of Acts and the Epistles describe the directives to
the church in the area of evangelism. The body of believers is
to saturate the community with biblical truths. Each person is
to witness. The new believers are to go to their own "household" first, immediately after being saved. The edification of
the church includes the constant awareness and study of the
Lord's mandate to "Go ye therefore, and teach all nations"
(Matt. 28:19) to "be witnesses unto me both in Jerusalem, and
in all Judea, and in Samaria, and unto the uttermost part of the
earth" (Acts 1:8).

Family

The family has a central place in the Bible (Eph. 5:24-33).
Such unity antedates the church, being a basic unit in the Old
Testament. Strong, united families form the backbone of the
church in edification, evangelism, and multiplication. Christian
families who serve the local church provide dynamic examples
of Christianity in their communities.

Structures

A careful study of the New Testament provides the forms
and structures as a means to biblical ends. Just as God has
spoken through the inspired Word, He has given us truth that
is absolute and "never changing." Christians believe in a God
who is eternal and a Savior who is the same "yesterday and
today, and forever" (Heb. 13:8). Often we tend to confuse
forms, patterns, structures, and ways of doing things to become just as sacred as biblical theology.

Ethnic churches must be creative in determining the fre-
quency, time, place, format, and so forth, for the gathering of
the believers. The compatibility of the organizational structure

and methods in the particular ethnic group will enhance the growth and multiplication of the church within the context of the people.

Leadership

The leaders of the first-century church came from among the people. They represented various traits and educational achievements. They were people called of God to serve. The tasks of these leaders were to manage (1 Tim. 3:4) their family and the family of God, the church. In 1 Peter 5:1-3, the leader is exhorted to shepherd the flock of God, not in an authoritarian manner, but as servants. Paul made specific mention that "The laborer is worthy of his reward" (1 Tim. 5:18). The leader is admonished to contextually "Study to show thyself approved unto God, . . . rightly dividing the word of truth" (2 Tim. 2:15).

Cultural Awareness

The New Testament did not ignore cultures. Jesus Christ revealed Himself in a cultural context. Culture is a reality of life. The ethnic church and the twentieth-century church must not ignore culture. Culture is a significant factor in the formulation of a biblical and contemporary philosophy of ministry. The growth of the church depends upon a strategy and methodology that is relevant, practical, and workable in changing cultural patterns.

The ethnic church, as well as the traditional church, must develop a perspective of the changing cultural and linguistic patterns of the American society. The contemporary church, whether ethnic or traditional, if it plans to meet the needs of the people, must learn to penetrate culture(s) just as the New Testament church penetrated the culture(s) of its day.

Denominationalism

Denominations seeking to evangelize America and the world, whether yuppies, poor, professionals, ethnics, or the segmentation of other groups, need to focus their programs at the segmented groups. Unfortunately, there is a tendency toward uniformity; to do more of the same when faced with problems and/or decline.

The philosophy of language missions to share the gospel within the context of the people, in a culturally comfortable setting, and in the language of the people is compatible with the American mosaic mission field.

Southern Baptist Mosaic

The validity of the continually emerging philosophy of the Southern Baptist Convention's Program of Language Missions, that respects people's dignity and responsibility for self-determination under God, can best be attested to by the growth and multidimensional approach. This philosophy began to evolve in the early 1950s with the election by the Home Mission Board of Dr. Loyd Corder as director of Hispanic work in Texas, New Mexico, and Arizona. Under Corder's leadership, the Mexican Baptist Children's Home, the Mexican Baptist Bible Institute (now the Hispanic Baptist Theological Seminary) in San Antonio, Texas, and the Valley Baptist Academy in Harlingen, Texas, were established. The process toward indigenous churches began with the School of Prophets which was begun to equip Spanish-speaking pastors. The gradual involvement of the state convention and local churches in evangelizing language-culture people resulted in the Home Mission Board's election of Corder to become secretary (director) of language missions.

In the mid 1950s Gerald B. Palmer was elected by the Home Mission Board to lead language missions work in New Mexico, where emphasis was given to the development of Bible study groups in the environment of the Spanish and Indian people.

I became a member of The Baptist General Convention of Texas staff, serving primarily among Hispanics. My election in

1965 as the first ethnic on the staff of the Home Mission Board brought three men—Corder, Palmer, and me—together. In 1966 Palmer and I worked together to establish a missiological foundation.

My election by the Home Mission Board to direct the Program of Language Missions was a historic first for Southern Baptists. An ethnic, American-Mexican, would lead a Southern Baptist Convention program. This program had the largest budget in the agency, supervised the largest number of missionary personnel, and managed property located throughout our nation, in Panama, Cuba, and Puerto Rico.

Thus Corder sought to improve the mission work and create a climate of concern for language-culture people. Palmer led in permitting creativity and encouraging flexibility in moving from a highly subsidized to an indigenous church. I have provided leadership in ethnic church planting and the catalytic role in the involvement of the various programs and agencies to focus their emphasis toward the development of ethnic churches, leadership training, contextual language materials, et cetera.

The Southern Baptist Convention agencies are directed to evangelizing, equipping, involving, assisting, and developing the ethnic segment of Southern Baptists. The following agencies and seminaries have elected ethnics to their staffs because of their ability to enhance the work of the agency. They are the: Home Mission Board, Sunday School Board, Woman's Missionary Union, Annuity Board, Foreign Mission Board, Brotherhood Commission, and Southern, Southwestern, New Orleans, and Golden Gate Seminaries.

Other agencies have assigned a person to give guidance to their involvement in this area of Southern Baptist work. Numerous ethnic people have been elected by the Southern Baptist Convention to serve on the Boards of various agencies. These serve, not because they are ethnics, but because they have a contribution to make toward the work of the agency to which they have been elected. The Southern Baptist Convention is, perhaps, the most cosmopolitan religious body in America, if not in the world. Each week Southern Baptists, representing 101 ethnic groups and 97 American Indian tribes within the United States and its territories, study the Bible and worship in 98 different languages in addition to American English.

The following charts reflect the involvement, contributions, support, concern, and so forth, by all Southern Baptist agencies and constituencies in their efforts to evangelize, congregationalize, and minister among mosaic Americans. Southern Baptists' greatest achievement is cooperation and God's leadership. These charts provide a brief overview of the Southern Baptist mosaic.

Chart A Southern Baptist Mosaic, Language Usage
Chart B Language Congregations/Units
Chart C Selected Urban Area
Chart D Language Communication Centers and Ministries
Chart E Contextual Language Materials
Chart F Refugee Resettlement
Chart G Decade of Ethnic Church Growth

The uniqueness of Southern Baptist polity and the centrality of the Bible has permitted Southern Baptists to imbue the ethnic segment of American society with the love of Jesus Christ. America is a mission field that must be penetrated, cultivated, and harvested.

Notes

1. Romo, 188.
2. *Missiology: An International Review,* "A Transcultural Gospel," (Scottdale, Pa.: American Society of Missiology, Oct. 1981), vol. 9, no. 4, 466.
3. "Guide for Establishing Ethnic Congregations," (Atlanta: Home Mission Board, 1978).

SOUTHERN BAPTIST MOSAIC
LANGUAGE USAGE

Categories	Ethnic Groups	Languages & Dialects
American Indians	1 (97 Tribes & Sub-Tribes)	22 (12 Language Families)
Asian Indian	10	10
Asian (Other)	16	23
Caribbean	3	3
Deaf	1	2
European	25	22
Hispanic	20	6
Latin American	1	1
Middle Eastern	14	6
Sub-Sahara African	10	3
Total	101	98

Source: Baptist state convention reports.

LANGUAGE CONGREGATIONS/UNITS, 1990

Ethnic Groups		Congregations/Units
American Indian		492
Asian		1,263
Cambodian	83	
Chinese	174	
Filipino	284	
Japanese	50	
Korean	435	
Laotian	110	
Samoan	8	
Thai	8	
Vietnamese	99	
Other	12	
Asian Indian		16
Caribbean		166
Deaf		697
European		207
Hispanic		2,612
Middle Eastern		56
Multiethnic		96
Sub-Sahara African		19
Total SBC Language Units		5,624

Source: Tabulation of Fields report from state conventions, Language Church Extension Division, HMB, 1990.

SELECTED URBAN AREAS

City	SBC Churches	Ethnic SBC Congregations	Percent Ethnic Congregations	Percent Ethnic Population
Atlanta, Ga.	108	21	19%	33%
Baltimore, Md.	56	6	11%	45%
Boston, Mass.	37	21	57%	38%
Buffalo, N.Y.	20	2	10%	50%
Charlotte, N.C.	88	8	9%	27%
Chicago, Ill.	114	40	35%	61%
Cincinnati, Ohio	51	2	4%	40%
Cleveland, Ohio	30	7	23%	44%
Columbus, Ohio	62	6	10%	32%
Dallas-Ft. Worth, Texas	374	201	54%	40%
Denver, Co.	48	11	23%	46%
Detroit, Mich.	40	8	20%	48%
Greensboro, N.C.	50	1	2%	27%
Hartford, Conn.	18	10	56%	46%
Houston, Texas	269	156	58%	56%
Kansas City, Mo.	115	21	18%	32%
Los Angeles, Calif.	327	208	64%	78%
Miami/Ft. Lauderdale/ West Palm Beach, Fla.	170	125	74%	79%
Minneapolis/St. Paul, Minn.	16	7	44%	38%
Nashville, Tenn.	120	10	8%	21%
New Orleans, La.	64	23	36%	54%
New York, N.Y.	113	62	55%	73%
Norfolk, Va.	63	5	8%	38%
Oklahoma City, Okla.	127	18	14%	30%
Philadelphia, Pa.	30	10	33%	46%
Phoenix, Ariz.	89	32	36%	50%
Pittsburgh, Pa.	20	1	5%	40%
Portland, Ore.	56	8	14%	31%
Rochester, N.Y.	11	2	18%	38%
Sacramento, Calif.	48	9	19%	50%
Salt Lake City, Utah	18	9	50%	27%
San Antonio, Texas	119	53	45%	90%
San Diego, Calif.	73	26	36%	59%
San Francisco, Calif.	81	23	28%	64%
Seattle/Tacoma, Wash.	59	15	25%	36%
St. Louis, Mo.	97	18	19%	41%
Tampa/St. Petersburg, Fla.	131	16	12%	38%
Washington, D.C.	64	22	34%	48%
Honolulu, Hawaii	22	10	45%	79%
Total	3,398	1,233	36%	45%

Sources: "Measuring the Results of Mega Focus Cities, 1982 to 1990," Clay Price, Research Division, Home Mission Board, SBC, July 1990, pp. 31-32; State Language Missions Program Leaders; U.S. Census Bureau.

LANGUAGE COMMUNICATION CENTERS

| | | Broadcasts | | | |
| | | Languages | | Stations | |
Language	Periodicals	Radio	TV	Radio	TV
Spanish	9	18	5	275	30
Polish	1				
Hungarian	1				
Romanian	1				
Korean	2				
Chinese	1				
Vietnamese	1				
Indonesian	1				
Italian	1				
English	14				
Dactylology	12				
American Indian	9				
Laotian	1				
Haitian	1				
Multilingual	4				
Bilingual	10				
Ukrainian	1				
Total	70	18	5	275	30

MINISTRIES

Church Related Weekly Units (est.)	5,472

Leadership Development

Ethnic Leadership Development Centers and Branches	80
Enrollment	1,500
Ethnic Groups	15
Languages	12
Continuing Education Units (granted for 800 participants)	1,700

Source: Tabulation of field reports, Language Church Extension Division, Home Mission Board.

CONTEXTUAL LANGUAGE MATERIALS

Southern Baptist agencies, in the efforts to focus their programs to meet the needs of ethnic/language-culture congregations, publish contextual language materials. The chart indicates the number of languages in which materials are printed.

SBC Agency	Number of Languages
Woman's Missionary Union	9
Brotherhood	2
Sunday School Board	10
Home Mission Board	10
Annuity Board	5
Stewardship Commission	3

REFUGEE RESETTLEMENT, 1975-1990
by Southern Baptist Churches

I.	Refugee cases assisted	10,280
	Persons resettled	47,586

II. Ministries provided

Type of Ministry	Churches Providing Ministry
English Language Skills	51
Medical Assistance	40
Employment Assistance	39
Housing Assistance	32
Clothing	29
Transportation	29
Furniture	23
Food	22
School Enrollment	21
Driver Training	22
Secure Social Security Number	17
How to Shop	12
Use of Social Services	11
Legal/Tax Assistance	5
Letters and Paper Work	5
Adult Education	3
Total	361

III.	Congregations Planted	968
IV.	Volunteers Involved	16,702
V.	Total Value of Goods/Cash/Services	$220,709,366

Source: Delbert G. Fann, "A Statistical Summary of Local Southern Baptist Assistance and Ministries to Refugees 1984-1990." Unpublished report, Language Church Extension Division, Home Mission Board, June 10, 1991.

DECADE OF ETHNIC CHURCH GROWTH
1980-1989

<u>Growth: 1980-1989</u>

Number of Congregations	142.9%
Baptisms Per Year	62.5%
Baptism Ratio (1989)	1:13.0
Bible Study Enrollment	94.6%
Cooperative Program Gifts	191.0%
Total Mission Gifts	170.4%
Church Income to Missions (1989)	8.0%
Woman's Missionary Union	52.9%
Brotherhood	87.5%

ETHNIC CONGREGATIONS
Church and Church-Type

	Increase in Congregations	Increase in Membership	Increase in Bible Study	Increase in Cooperative Program
American Indian	38.3%	21%	31.1%	44%
Asian	556%	384%	506.1%	550%
Caribbean	450%	225%	762.9%	801%
Deaf	146%	129%	234%	24%
European	362%	436%	437.5%	620%
Hispanic	87%	54%	43.3%	125%
Middle Eastern	360%	404%	514%	1,424%
Sub-Saharan	283%	228%	158%	1,681%

COMPARATIVE GROWTH
Percent Change: 1980-1989

	Number of Churches	Total Members	Number of Baptisms
Total SBC	+5.45%	+9.60%	-18.30%
Language	+142.86%	+93.73%	+62.51%
SBC Less Language	-2.99%	+8.71%	-20.84%

6 Strategies for Ethnic America

Modern strategy, "the art of a calculated risk,"[1] is a plan designed to achieve an objective and may be dated to the nineteenth century. "The Bible points to the care with which Moses prepared his operations, an early form of planning."[2]

God in His divine strategy sent His son to reconcile (basic objective) all (numerical) men to Him. Jesus has commissioned, "You shall be My witnesses both in Jerusalem, and in all Judea and Samaria, and even to the remotest part of the earth" (Acts 1:8, NASB). This presents a geographical strategy. The Book of Acts further delineates the design of God's divine strategy. The disciples were (are) given the task of developing a geographically segmented strategy. The second chapter of Acts describes the diversity, both ethnically and linguistically (vv. 5-11), of the known world and its various components. Paul and Barnabas were recalled to Jerusalem to discuss the deculturalization of the gospel by sharing it with the Gentiles. The Jerusalem Council further segmented the cultural and linguistic components of God's strategy. Philip proclaimed the message to the Ethiopian. Peter went, at God's insistence, to Cornelius, the Roman centurion. The cultural heritage of the people becomes another segment of God's plan to redeem all persons unto Himself.

The divine strategy, in addition to segmentation, denotes the tactics that are to be used in proclaiming the biblical message of reconciliation. Some tactics were the healing of the hemorrhaging woman, giving a drink of water to the Samaritan woman, feeding the five thousand, and other such ministries that led people to acknowledge Christ as Lord.

The church denomination is called to develop its own strategy designed to include every segment of the people and tactics to achieve the basic objective, to bring all men into a personal relationship with Jesus Christ.

A national strategy calls for a pragmatic plan whose segmented components are designed to include all the cultural and geographical dimensions of the nation. This strategy must give emphasis to the study of mankind, anthropology, and human relationship with the Creator. It gives specific attention to various cultural uniquenesses, linguistic diversification, physiological qualities, philosophy of life, as well as cultural and linguistic similarities. Consideration is also to be given to the numerical data, demographic patterns, cultural cohesiveness, geographical boundaries, and transitional aspects of life. The strategy must seek to assist churches, associations, and state conventions to carry out the Great Commission.

Various strategies and plans should include channels for communication, approaches, programs to be implemented, and tactics that will address themselves to all persons. Types of personnel needed are determined so they may be deployed in keeping with the strategy. Investment of resources needs serious consideration lest the recipients become dependent. Various elements of church growth holography (Greek, "whole message") provide a better understanding of the growth of the congregation in relation to the contextual, cultural, and numerical dimensions.

Strategies should call not only for development of persons but for the empowering by the Holy Spirit. These are necessary to achieve God's basic objective to reconcile all persons unto Himself.

Strategies should be developed by each state, association, and urban area. The following is a planning document that has been used effectively. The Language Church Extension Division has had a strategy design for each state since the mid-1970s. The Microcosmic Urban Strategy was developed in the early 1980s, thus providing input from the Mega Focus Cities to the state convention planning process. Both of the following documents will be helpful in developing a national strategy.

Microcosmic Urban Strategy

Objective: To develop a pragmatic strategy design in an ethnolinguistic contextual approach that is multidimensional in an urban strategy.

Historically, "The early evolution of urban communities occurred between the sixth and first millennium B.C. in widely separated parts of southern Asia."[3] These communities provided shelter, protection, social arrangements, and supporting activities that have gradually evolved into twentieth-century urban scenes across the nation. "The urban scene is the last frontier for missions."[4]

Biblical Overview

The Bible magnifies the city. It tells of God's servants following their call to care for the city. Abraham prayed for Sodom. Moses oversaw construction of the cities of Egypt. Jonah was sent to Nineveh. Jeremiah wept for the captives in Babylon. Isaiah, in response to God's call, asked, "How long?" and God answered, "Until the cities be wasted without inhabitant, and the houses without man, and the land be utterly desolate" (Isa. 6:11).

Jesus was born and grew up in Bethlehem and Nazareth. He wept for the multitudes in Jerusalem. The early church was launched in the city, as the apostles tarried in Jerusalem to be "endued with power from on high" (Luke 24:49).

Paul, the missionary, recognized culture as an invaluable vehicle for the communication process. A Roman citizen, he chose to be a Jew among Jews (see 1 Cor. 9:19-22). Paul's missionary journeys took him to the urban areas of the known world. People of diverse cultures, who spoke a variety of languages, were those with whom he sought to communicate the gospel.

Urban Ethnicity

People of diverse backgrounds continue to transform the face of urban America. Thirty-one cities increased in ethnic population between 1970 and 1980. In New York, the historic home of immigrants, one in four persons is foreign born. Asians are the stabilizing influence in the city. Astoria, in Queens, New York, has the third largest Greek community in the world.

"The pluralism of the nation is so diverse that Cambodian is spoken in Houston; Hindi in Philadelphia; Arabic in Atlanta; and Haitian Creole in Jersey City."[5] These are only some of the 636[6] languages through which Americans communicate.

"The ethnicity of Chicago has increased 100% in a decade. Detroit is proud of its ethnic diversity, which includes 200,000 Arabs. Los Angeles has become the mecca for people from so many lands that the police speak 42 languages. People with an Asian Pacific heritage have doubled. Eighty-two percent of the foreign trade in Los Angeles is with Pacific nations."[7] Los Angeles, perhaps, has the largest illegal/undocumented population in America, if not in the world, with 200,000 to 300,000 Central Americans in addition to others. "Ethnic communities create neighborhoods that add flavor, diversity and stability"[8] to the American way of life.

The heartbeat of urban America is ethnic. "In 13 of the

nation's 20 largest metropolitan areas, the combined ethnic and racial minorities comprise more than 50 percent of the total population."[9] The "combined population of the 38 metropolitan areas with a population of more than a million represent 40 percent of the nation's population."[10] Yet only "15 percent of the Southern Baptist churches are located in the 38 metropolitan areas."[11] Everett Anthony, director of missions in Chicago, has said that "the ethnicity of America's cities contributes to the plurality that baffles many Southern Baptists."[12] He urges Southern Baptists to "embrace diversity."[13]

Urban Strategy

Microcosmic Urban Strategy is an effort to develop a pragmatic plan, with components adaptable to the many language-culture variances of urban areas. This strategy seeks to help existing churches understand the microcosmic dimensions of language-culture people in urban settings, ministering in microcosmic transitional communities, establishing new language-culture units as a part of its ongoing program, and using their facilities for maximum transcultural outreach. It seeks to establish new units by utilizing the microcosmic dimensions as channels for bringing language-culture people into a right relationship with Jesus Christ, gradually formalizing culturally and linguistically comfortable, organizational units and/or language-culture churches. This permits the new units to see themselves in their microcosmic dimensions.

Basis

The Microcosmic Urban Strategy seeks to implement the call for commitment to the task as given by our Lord, Jesus Christ. It is an effort to be "a witness unto all nations" (Greek, ethnics) (Matt. 24:14). This is in response to the command, "Go ye therefore, and teach all nations, baptizing them in the name of the Father, and of the Son, and of the Holy Ghost: Teaching them to observe all things whatsoever I have commanded you: and, lo, I am with you always, even unto the end of the world" (Matt. 28:19-20). In other words, leave—go to all ethnic groups everywhere and "preach the gospel to every creature" (Mark 16:15). Preach to the whole cosmos, which includes every microcosm.

Principles

New Testament church growth principles, recorded in the second chapter of Acts, must be applied in the ethnolinguistic context of the people. These principles are: 1. Penetration; 2. Spiritual nurture; 3. Leaders from among the people; 4. Communication in the language of the people; 5. Economic stability; 6. Adequate facilities; 7. Multiplication.

Concepts

Church-growth concepts have "developed slowly through experience."[14] They originated as thoughts or ideas that motivate learning. The pluralistic diversity of the nation's inhabitants calls for experiences that can be expanded and implemented in diverse contexts. The concepts listed are designed to permit flexibility that is in keeping with the objectives of the strategy.

The Laser Thrust concept is expanded by the use of these approaches:

1. Research/Survey/Compilation—seeks to do seed-sowing, compile data, gauge response and future planning.
2. Motivation/Action/Conservation—seeks to discover, enlist, motivate, equip leaders and disciple recent converts.
3. Penetration/Saturation/Harvest—seeks to ingather new converts and establish new units. Mass communication and group meetings are utilized extensively.
4. Cultural/Sowing/Selling—may be used in lieu of, or as a supplement to, approach three. It uses music, drama, art,

and athletics to prepare for sowing seeds and "selling" gospel concepts.

These may be used in a cycling pattern—thus being able to provide the flexibility and creativity needed to accomplish the task of the Laser Thrust concept.

The Catalytic Church Growth concept should be enlarged to include these functions:

1. Catalytic Cycling—the catalytic missionary assigned to a specific area, with the understanding that there will be a regular evaluation of the task. The task may call for the missionary to be cycled into another responsibility, so that current needs may be met as the structure of the ethnic community changes and the work develops.

2. Catalytic Lending—urban areas often call for the assignment of several catalytic personnel, each with a specific language and cultural expertise, serving a selected area. This function permits the "lending" of catalytic personnel to assist other areas needing expertise for specified functions. This is done in cooperation with the person assigned to the area needing assistance.

3. Catalytic Coordinator—the person who provides leadership to all catalytic missionaries. This avoids duplications, provides a cooperative thrust and correlates the lending system among various geographical areas.

Kaleidoscopic Church Growth permits the church, with facilities located in a culturally transitional area, to minister and witness. The kaleidoscopic church grows in a variety of lifestyles, economic variances, educational levels, ethnic diversities, linguistic channels, cultural uniquenesses, geographical barriers, and living conditions. It permits various groups to work cooperatively, yet be autonomous. Thus each group retains its own identity, language, and cultural uniqueness.

The Kairos (Action Now) concept is designed to develop a strategy in an urban setting and equip leaders in both practicum and academia. Personnel are selected for a limited time to verify the ethnicity, initiate new work, enlist and equip leaders, develop contextual language materials, and design a strategy.

Design

The actual design of Microcosmic Urban Strategy must include at least seven factors. These factors should be considered in light of the anthropological study and data gathered on the particular urban area. These factors are: 1. Geographical, 2. Denominational, 3. Anthropological, 4. Socioeconomic, 5. Historical, 6. Relational, and 7. Responsive quotient.

Resources

To a great extent, missionary strategy is people who have a personal experience with Jesus Christ, who want to share that experience with others, who are called to "go" tell the story of their experience, and who give of their "worldly" accomplishments in order for others to go tell the good news. Thus mission strategy must have human and financial resources to be implemented. The initial investment(s) may come from outside the "target" area that is being evangelized. The investments should be gradually reduced as the new groups of believers is led to assume responsibility for their own work. They should begin immediately to participate in tithing and gifts to missions.

The mission field basically contains resources necessary for the growth of the local church. It is imperative that practical plans for the reduction of financial assistance be developed together with the local group of believers. Such a plan, however, should never give preference to financial reduction. It should give priority to the need for continuing a witness wherever such is needed. In each instance, the local group should be led to assume the major responsibilities, in keeping with their potential.

Personnel Development

The magnitude of the urban areas, their unique cultural diversities and mobility must be considered in the deployment of missionary personnel. People assigned to the various areas should have a working knowledge of the language(s) and an awareness of cultural values and characteristics.

Missionary personnel are deployed to establish and develop the mission field. These missionaries should quickly develop leaders from among the people, guiding them to assume leadership responsibilities. This missionary role continually changes as new work is begun. Leaders are developed and new opportunities for witness and ministry become a challenge. The work of the missionary never ceases, but continually changes to meet the changing dimensions of the mission field.

The use of various church growth concepts calls for at least five categories of personnel. A position description, with specific responsibilities and flexible assignments that permit creativity, must be prepared in keeping with the strategy for each particular area to be served. These personnel categories are: 1. Messengers of the Word (employed pastor/layperson); 2. Pastoral; 3. General missionary (not otherwise classified); 4. Catalytic missionaries; and 5. Catalytic coordinator.

People assigned to the mission field must have a working relationship with the participating mission agencies and the local association, and/or churches. This will make possible the coordination that helps achieve the basic goals of the Microcosmic Urban Strategy.

Measurement

Metrology, the science of measurement, is of fundamental importance in determining the success of Microcosmic Urban

Strategy. The measurement must be based upon the achievement of objectives of the strategy in relation to human activity. Measurement includes both quantitative and qualitative achievements. Tangible measurement includes numerical, financial, outreach activities, type of ministries, organizational structures, programs, and actual growth.

Intangible measurement must be evaluated in terms of the particular language-culture groups, geographical relationships, and socioeconomic status as relates to the acceptability by the people. The response of the language-culture group to the gospel should be considered in terms of their socioreligious background.

Analysis

Analysis, to a great extent, seeks to extend our knowledge and remove problems and perplexities, which are not the result of ignorance of fact, but of conceptual confusion and misunderstanding. It is a procedure of conceptual clarification. Analysis should give attention to: 1. Programming achievements; 2. Anthropological pluralism; 3. Data update; 4. Personnel development; 5. Church growth patterns; 6. Invested resources; and 7. Cooperation evaluation.

Each area should be analyzed separately, yet considered a part of the strategy. The result of such a study will greatly contribute to the updating of the Microcosmic Urban Strategy.

Modern missiology calls for a scientific approach to the mission field. Microcosmic Urban Strategy will not guarantee growth. It will provide a sense of direction for making disciples, establishing new congregations and ministries, selecting priorities, and future growth.

Mega Focus/Metro Thrust

The urban areas challenge Southern Baptists to replace their cultural myopia with a vision of "individuals who perceive themselves to have a common affinity for one another—an affinity based upon language and culture"[15] and who cherish their heritage. American urban complexity calls for creative approaches that permit the contextualization (interweaving) of the gospel into changing cultural patterns of urbanites.

Baptists located in the urban areas will want to give attention to the suggested and proven process for developing a language missions strategy for America's urban areas.

The strategy planning group will want to consult with the associational Missions Development program committee in developing a language missions strategy. It would be the part of wisdom for the ethnic/language-culture congregations and leaders to be encouraged to become participatory partners in the planning.

The suggested planning process and the preparation of the documents (app. A-C) provide the opportunity for "input" into the state and Home Mission Board planning process and priorities. (app. D is the response; app. E is the flow chart.)

Prepare

Preparation is essential to a successful endeavor. The associational Missions Development program provides leadership in developing a Microcosmic Urban Strategy.

1. Initiate Research—Research on the ethnicity of the area should be initiated to discover information available and that is needed. The area or regional planning commission, Chamber of Commerce and/or educational institutions are valuable sources of information. There may be ethnic organizations that have similar purposes and that are more aware of ethnic dimensions. County welfare and special service agencies also are valuable sources of information. These can help identify community problems relating to ethnic people and suggest the relationship of their programs to churches and associations. Be

alert to information concerning ethnic influence and future plans to meet all people's needs.

2. Secure Maps—Maps should be secured from the planning commission or a research organization, preferably size 30"x 43". These large maps should have the census tracts, natural boundaries, main roads, and other pertinent information. If overlays are available, secure these also. Ethnicity information may be compiled as shown in appendixes A and B.

3. Contact Organizations—Ethnic organizations, active in the area, should be contacted. These groups are well acquainted with needs, problems, population density, and influences of ethnic people in the area. This provides opportunities for meeting leaders from among the people. Mailing lists and so forth may be available when genuine interest is demonstrated.

4. Begin to Map/Chart Data—Charts and maps are an excellent way to graph statistics and other information. Data on ethnicity should be charted on a census map, demonstrating the ethnic concentration as of the last census. Use charts to show the ethnic influence according to other information gathered thus far.

5. Prepare Overlays—Overlays will enhance a visual understanding of existing circumstances, trends, and opportunities. These should be ordered with the 30 x 43 inch maps. If not available, purchase clear acetate to use over the maps. Develop a legend for churches, ethnic organizations, businesses, and so forth. Locate these on an overlay. Then, using another overlay, use a color scheme to chart the ethnic density. This color scheme is suggested: (1) American Indian (North American)—red; (2) Asian and Pacific—blue; (3) European—yellow; (4) Hispanic—green; (5) Middle Eastern—orange; (6) Asian Indian—purple; (7) Caribbean—silver; (8) Sub-Sahara—

gold; (9) Deaf—brown; (10) Anglo—white; (11) Transition—dot.
Other overlays can be used to map the penetration strategy and development of a language missions strategy.
Other pertinent information also may be charted.

6. Compile a History—A brief history of ethnic/language-
culture work in the area should be compiled. The when,
how, why, where, and by whom will provide an historical
overview.

7. Develop a Plan—Using an overlay on the map indicating
the ethnicity, develop a plan for sharing the gospel
contextually. These factors should be considered in developing a pragmatic plan: (1) Census data; (2) Ethnic
population density; (3) Geographical relationship of ethnic communities and cultural cohesiveness; and (4) Selected target groups.

Consider

Consider the approaches that should be undertaken to develop a strategy. The following approaches are efforts to
strengthen various aspects of ethnic/language-culture church
growth. The Language Church Extension Division will seek to
assist in these areas:

1. New Work—Establishing new ethnic/language-culture
congregations, using various approaches recommended
by the Language Church Extension Division.
Ethnic Groups—Language-culture groups, self-identified
in the United States, for example, Chinese, German,
Hispanic, and so forth.
Laser Thrust—Contextual language missions approach
to penetrate selected areas, communicate the gospel,
discover natural leaders, establish new congregations,
and strengthen churches in transitional areas.

Concepts—These concepts provide for carrying out various approaches to reach ethnic America with the gospel:

(1) Ethnic Church Growth—Establishing and developing ethnic/language-culture congregations:

(2) Transcultual Outreach—Assisting Baptist churches in ministering among ethnic/language-culture people, who are within reach of the church, through church programs, organizations and facilities, adapting these to particular needs.

(3) Catalytic Church Growth—The concept is one based upon the idea of a change agent in chemistry. Catalytic Church Growth permits a person to work among several ethnic groups at the same time (1) to plant churches; (2) to assist existing churches to grow; (3) to discover new contextual methods; (4) to enlist, equip, and undergird lay preachers; (5) to develop contextual language materials; and (6) to work cooperatively with local mission entities.

(4) Kaleidoscopic—Permits proclamation, worship, leadership development, ministry, and missions in changing ethnic patterns, while retaining the transitional community's cultural uniqueness.

2. Leadership—Indigenous leaders working in a contextual environment.

Catalytic—Appointed missionary personnel, serving an ethnic/language-culture group or groups within an assigned region or geographical area. Their primary responsibilities are to discover, enlist, train, and undergird ethnic people serving local congregations.

Mentorship—A two-year program for people with potential for leadership to develop their skills.

Kairos—A three-year term of service to assist in developing a language-missions strategy for a particular area.

Pastoral—A pastor serving a self-supporting, self-sustaining, or locally supported congregation.

Messenger of the Word—A layperson or minister serving voluntarily as pastor of a local ethnic/language-culture congregation.

3. Contextual Language Materials—Materials in the language of the people, with content, style, and art design culturally appropriate for the ethnic group's context.

4. Awareness—Creating an awareness of language-culture people and language missions.

    Language Missions Day—The second Sunday in August is designated Language Missions Day on the Southern Baptist Convention Calendar of Activities.

    Language Missions Opportunities—Discover and emphasize opportunities for service.

5. Special Groups—Groups among whom ministries may be developed.

    Internationals—People in the United States for a limited period of time; nonimmigrants, with a temporary visa, include tourists, sea and air crews, professionals, and diplomats.

    Refugees—People compelled to live outside their homeland, some of whom seek to resettle in the United States.

    Undocumented—People entering and residing in the United States illegally.

6. Projects—Bible distribution and special campaigns:

    Bible Distribution—Specific projects to distribute language Scriptures.

    Special Campaigns—Specific efforts to provide an emphasis not being given attention for example, evangelistic crusades, and so forth.

7. Church Development—These programs would contribute to developing language-culture congregations: (1) Bible study; (2) Religious education; (3) Leadership

training; (4) Mission education; (5) Stewardship; and (6) Music.
8. Additional Approaches—Other suggested approaches that would enhance sharing the gospel among language-culture people should be considered and recommended.

Recommend

The associational missions development program (Associational Missions Committee) should seek to secure the participatory involvement of ethnic/language-culture people. Otherwise it may be involved in encouraging "Manifest Destiny." The document, "Strategy Recommendations," was designed to assist in preparing these language missions recommendations (see app. C).

The Language Church Extension Division should receive this document, including the recommendations, at least two weeks prior to the mega focus/metro thrust meeting.

Strategy Participation

The Language Church Extension Division will review recommendations from associations in keeping with the assignment of the Convention and goals, guidelines and policies of the Home Mission Board. Participation will be in keeping with the language-missions national strategy, state convention priorities, and availability of funds (see app. D).

Strategy participation will be discussed during the mega focus/metro thrust response meeting. The final commitment will be in keeping with the planning process.

Microcosmic Urban Strategy

Mega Focus Cities may be, in essence, the last frontier of missions in America. Plans developed during this emphasis will be incorporated into the Microcosmic Urban Strategy.

The Microcosmic Urban Strategy is an effort to develop a

master plan with components adaptable to the many ethnic/ language-culture variances of metropolitan areas. Modern missiology calls for a scientific approach to the mission field. Such a strategy will not guarantee growth, but it will provide a sense of direction for making disciples and initiating new congregations, ministries, and future growth.

Five-Year Strategy Plans

Planning Process

Basically, the planning process for language churches involves five cyclical steps. Each step is a progression toward field implementation.

I.   Statement of Missions/Purpose
     This process of thinking through, discussing, and making statements about the reason for a program's existence provides an important means of organizing and clarifying those elements at work creating the future.

II. Determination of Environment
     Deciding what characteristics of the environment, or present situation, that directly affect the program of work, is step two. This involves the collection and interpretation of data. The purpose directs this process and may be refined by it. This is to include census data, historical review, and church-growth analysis.

III. Program Projections
     The state plan for developing new language work and strengthening existing work is step three.

IV. State Strategy Design
     The state plan for developing a contextual, geographical, and financial implementation of the language-missions strategy is step four.

V.   Evaluation
     While a final evaluation determines if the goals have

been met and the objective reached, the evaluation process is not restricted to the last stages of the planning process. Evaluation must take place in each step, and appropriate revision or refinement should take place on a continuing basis.

Language/Ethnic Strategy Plans—Five Years

 I. Statement of Purpose of Language Missions Program
 II. Environment
    A. Data
       1. State
       2. County
       3. Consolidated Metropolitan Statistical Area (CMSA)
       4. Primary Metropolitan Statistical Area (PMSA)
       5. Standard Metropolitan Statistical Area (SMSA)
       6. Places of 50,000 or more
       7. Places of 10,000 or more
       8. Others (refugees, undocumented, media, et cetera)
       9. Ethnic organizations
    B. Historical Review
    C. Church-Growth Analysis
    D. Personnel Categories
    E. Properties
    F. Present Work
       1. Map
       2. List previous work
       3. List previous 1-5 years
       4. Classification of fields
    G. Mission Gifts
 III. Program Projections
    A. New Work
       1. Location (map overlay)
       2. Ethnic groups (map overlay)

   3. Type of new work (chart)
   4. Resources (local, state, national)
B. Awareness
C. Leadership Development
D. Contextual Materials
E. Bible Distribution
F. Self-Support
G. Programming
   1. Bible study
   2. Leadership training
   3. Missions organizations
   4. Stewardship
IV. State Strategy Design
   A. Contextual (overlay—ethnic groups by color, see pp. 186-187)
   B. Geographical Design (map overlay)
      1. a. Congregations
            (1) Potential churches
            (2) Slow-developing churches
            (3) Mission churches
            (4) Preaching points
         b. Ministries
            (1) Refugees
            (2) Others
      2. Field Design
         a. Congregations
            (1) Potential churches
            (2) Slow-developing churches
            (3) Mission churches
            (4) Combined fields
         b. Geographical/Cultural
            (1) Regions
            (2) Urban areas
            (3) Associations

3. Relate to present entities
4. Deployment of personnel
5. Vacancies
C. Priorities Selected
   1. Home Mission Board—A.D. 2000
   2. Five-year priorities
   3. Annual priority card developed
V. Strategy Budget Statement
   The Five-Year Planning Process will be updated annually. Please refer to the Annual Language Church Extension Strategy Update. The strategy design reflects the state strategy as agreed upon by the state and the Home Mission Board. It serves as a guide for Board Actions.

"Leadership requires a great vision."[16] "Where there is no vision, the people perish" (Prov. 29:18). Leaders think of tomorrow. Planning permits us to look beyond the horizon. "Missionary strategy is never intended to be a substitute for the Holy Spirit."[17] Planning must include various cultural aspects of American society. It must anticipate the future, provide for alternatives, and above all, be focused to meet the needs of the people and their relationship to Jesus Christ. Planning, based upon known factors, provides the sense of direction for carrying out the Great Commission.

Notes

1. *Encyclopedia Britannica* (Chicago: William Benton Publisher, 1973), vol. 21, 289.
2. Ibid., 290.
3. Warren E. Preece, ed., *Encyclopedia Britannica* (Chicago: William Benton Publisher, 1980), vol. 5, 809.
4. Roger S. Greenway, *An Urban Strategy for Latin America* (Grand Rapids, Michigan: Baker Book House, 1973), 96.
5. *U.S. News and World Report* (Washington, D.C.: U.S. News and World Report, Inc., March 21, 1983), 49-53.

6. David B. Barrett, *World Christian Encyclopedia* (New York: Oxford University Press, 1982), 711.

7. *U.S. News and World Report,* 49-53.

8. *U.S. News and World Report,* 49-53.

9. David Wilkinson, *Urban Heartbeat* (Atlanta: Home Mission Board, 1981), 13.

10. Ibid., Wilkinson, 13.

11. Ibid., Wilkinson, 13.

12. Ibid., Wilkinson, 15.

13. Ibid., Wilkinson, 15.

14. Preece, vol. 5, 254.

15. Edward R. Dayton and David A. Fraser, *Planning Strategies for World Evangelization* (Grand Rapids: William B. Eerdmans Publishing Co., 1980), 37.

16. Richard Nixon, *Leaders,* (New York: Warner Books, Inc., 1982), 5.

17. C. Peter Wagner, *Frontiers in Missionary Strategy* (Chicago: Moody Press, 1971), 15.

ETHNICITY BY ASSOCIATION

Association_____

Total Ethnic Population _____

Total Association Population _____

Percent Ethnic _____

Ethnic Group	Ethnic Population	
Asian and Pacific		
Japanese		
Chinese		
Filipino		
Korean		
Asian Indian		
Vietnamese		
Hawaiian		
Guamanian		
Samoan		
Other		
American Indian (North America)		
Aleut		
Eskimo		
Caribbean		
Hispanic		
Mexican		
Puerto Rican		
Cuban		
Other		
Middle Eastern and North African		
Sub-Sahara Africa		
European (see next chart)		
Totals		
Deaf/Hearing Impaired		
Totals		

Obtain information from U.S. Census bulletins PC 80-1-B (state series). For European information consult PC 80-S1-10, which provides state information. Also consult city government, Chamber of Commerce, health and school institutions for specific information by county. Most documents should be found in public libraries.

Association_____

Ethnic Group	Foreign Born	Single Ancestry	Totals
Europeans			
Austrian			
Czechoslovakian			
Dutch			
English			
French			
German			
Greek			
Hungarian			
Irish			
Italian			
Norwegian			
Polish			
Portuguese			
Russian			
Scottish			
Swedish			
Ukrainian			
Welsh			
Yugoslavian			
Totals			

Appendix B

ETHNICITY BY COUNTIES

Association_____
Total Ethnic Population _____
Total Association Population _____
Percent Ethnic _____

Ethnic Group	County	County	County	County
Asian and Pacific				
Japanese				
Chinese				
Filipino				
Korean				
Asian Indian				
Vietnamese				
Hawaiian				
Guamanian				
Samoan				
Other				
American Indian				
North American				
Aleut				
Eskimo				
Caribbean				
Hispanic				
Mexican				
Puerto Rican				
Cuban				
Other				
Middle Eastern and North African				
Sub-Sahara African				
European (see next chart)				
Totals				
Deaf/Hearing Impaired				
Totals				

Obtain information from U.S. Census bulletins PC 80-1-B (state series). For European information consult PC 80-S1-10 that provides state information. Also consult city government, Chamber of Commerce, health and school institutions for specific information by county. Most documents should be found in public libraries.

Association_____

Ethnic Group	County	County	County	County
Europeans				
Austrian				
Czechoslovakian				
Dutch				
English				
French				
German				
Greek				
Hungarian				
Irish				
Italian				
Norwegian				
Polish				
Portuguese				
Russian				
Scottish				
Swedish				
Ukrainian				
Welsh				
Yugoslavian				
Other				
Totals				

Appendix C

MEGA FOCUS - STRATEGY RECOMMENDATIONS

State _____
City _____

Recommendations
Association _____
State _____
Language Church Extension Division _____

Approach	Priority	Goal	Action	Responsibility	Resources Needed
					Financial/Human
I. New Work					
II. Leadership					
III. Contextual Language Materials					
IV. Awareness					
V. Special Groups					

continued

MEGA FOCUS - STRATEGY RECOMMENDATIONS

State _____
City _____

Recommendations _____
Association _____
State _____
Language Church Extension Division _____

Approach	Priority	Goal	Action	Responsibility	Resources Needed
					Financial/Human
VI. Projects					
VII. Facilities					
VIII. Sponsorship					
IX. Training					
X. Church Development					
XI. Unusual Approaches					

_____ Date reviewed by state language missions director. Attach copy of strategy participation.

MEGA FOCUS - STRATEGY RECOMMENDATIONS

Recommendations
Association _____
State _____
Language Church Extension Division _____

Approach	Mega Focus	Planning/Priorities		Cost-Financial Participation				
		Assoc. Stra. Partic.				Cooperative Agreement		
	Funds	5 Years	State	Local	Association	State	HMB	Comments
I. New Work								
II. Leadership								
III. Contextual								
IV. Congregationalize								
V. Awareness								
VI. Special Groups								
VII. Projects								
VIII. Facilities								
IX. Sponsorship								
X. Church Development								

FLOW CHART
Mega Focus Metro Thrust

3 Years Before — Consult	2 Years Before — Prepare	1 Year Before — Penetrate, Compile and Recommend	Mega Focus Year — Select/Implement	1 Year After — Review Recommend	2 Years After — Implement
1. Consult with association, state, and Home Mission Board	1. Prepare maps/chart data	1. Penetrate with Laser Thrust	1. Implement approved projects	1. Review continuation of approved project	1. Implement-- approved priorities become part of Cooperative Agreement (State/HMB budget)
2. Request for Laser by association/state	2. Select target groups	2. Compile information	2. Recommend priorities by association -to state -to Language Church Extension Division (LCED) -LCED recommends to HMB	2. Recommend approval of priorities HMB	
3. Approve Laser request by Home Mission Board (HMB)	3. Complete data process by SRTI	3. Recommend strategy and priorities			
	4. Penetrate with Laser Thrust	4. Map associational strategy design			
		5. Identify associational projects/priorities			
		6. Approve Mega Focus projects			

7 The Waves of Time

The wind and water, with the passage of time, grind the mighty boulders into beautiful, soft, attractive sand. Sand that covers the beautiful beaches, which we all enjoy, was in all probability once large boulders.

The surfer goes to the beach to enjoy riding the waves until his destination, the beach, is reached. Every surfer strives to ride the waves on the surfboard, arriving on the beach standing up. The surfer studies the waves. He is aware of the various kinds of waves and, through experience, can estimate the speed of the waves and the velocity of the wind that propels them. In a sense, he knows the context of the ocean upon which he surfs—the depth, the bottom of the ocean, the direction(s) of the wind, the type of waves, the kinds of sand upon the beach, the approaches that must be made to reach the beach, and the dexterity of the sand on the beach. These are all important if the surfer is to be successful.

The surfer enters the ocean and swims to the area where the waves gradually form. He studies the waves carefully, noticing their trends. He chooses a wave, climbs on the surfboard, and carefully places his feet on it. His feet will anchor him to the surfboard, giving him stability. Once on the surfboard, the surfer must maintain his equilibrium in motion. To do otherwise can be disastrous. Rigidity can prove to be fatal. To stay on the surfboard provides a sense of achievement. There is personal satisfaction that he is accepting the challenge of the waves and the wind, and he is flexible (bends) if the goal is to be achieved. The surfer rides the waves that rise ten, fifteen feet above the sea. He has achieved great heights. From this height he looks beyond the horizon and thinks, *Look at me. I am the greatest surfer in the world. I am riding the mighty waves.* But, he must constantly remind himself that, although he has achieved great heights, they can be dangerous and treacherous. He must concentrate on reaching his objective, not upon his selfish achievement. To lessen his grip on the board or to cease giving attention to his equilibrium or stability will result in failure to reach the beautiful beach, all the time moving forward.

Throughout the entire time the surfer rides on the crest of the wave, there is satisfaction of achievement. Yet he must be careful and aware that a fall off the surfboard is both dangerous and imminent. The wave begins to lose its velocity and will probably not reach the beach. The surfer begins to look for another wave to which he can transfer that will take him all the way to the beach. He must find a wave headed in the right direction, whose velocity will carry him to his objective, the beach. The surfer must be ready, alert, flexible, and willing to move quickly as he makes the transition to the wave that will take him to the beautiful sand on the beach that was once a gigantic boulder.

Waves of Immigrants

The waves of time have brought immigrants to the beaches of our nation. This is a migration that began with the Conquistadores, followed by the Pilgrims, intensified by those from Latin America, and currently being impacted by those who come from the Pacific Rim nations. The song, "They're Comin' to America," is descriptive of the continual development of these United States. These new Americans, upon arrival, are faced with "four myths."

1. *All are welcomed.*—Early immigration policy kept out the undesirables—the "yellow horde," the "Mexican," and the Jewish children fleeing Nazi Germany. Preference was given to the European.
2. *Immigrants are huddled masses.*—Emma Lazarus, in her poem "Huddled Masses," describes the early European immigrant. The immigrant today is often wealthy, proud of his heritage, educated, and a professional. The port of entry is not Ellis Island, but LAX (Los Angeles) and MIA (Miami). Immigration has become "selective and optional, a challenge not a change, for exploitation not identification and for profit not prayer."[1]
3. *All men are our brothers.*—The myth is that all people are admitted, since ideological concerns have been removed from the American Alien Admission policy. The law has brought no change to policy. Asylum rates clearly indicate that Martina Navratilova and Hu Na, both tennis players, did not have to prove fear of persecution. However, there are Salvadorians, Haitians, and others in detention camps waiting to be sent home because they are neither professionals nor can they prove fear of persecution.
4. *All are equal!*—It is said that America is a melting pot where the English language is the "language" and the "Anglo" (European) culture is superior. In reality, there are 500 ethnic groups who daily speak 636 languages of which 26 are considered major languages. There are the nuclear ethnics, ethnic Americans, American ethnics, and the culturally aware ethnics.

Have you stopped to contemplate why God, in His divine plan, has brought the world to this part—our nation—of the North American continent? Or how, in a sense, He is helping us to carry out His commandment—to go to the nations (*ta ethne*) and preach the gospel?

On the Crest of the Wave

In the last quarter century Southern Baptists have risen to the crest of the wave in evangelizing ethnic America. Ethnic Southern Baptists have increased 142.8 percent in a decade in new congregations, a baptism ratio of one for every ten members, and gifts to missions through the Cooperative Program of 267.8 percent or over $4 million in 1989.

Our Borderless World

The movement of people across the borders of the world is almost invisible. People are global. " 'Global citizenship' " is no longer in the lexicon of futurologists."[2]

America has become a global mission field from which the gospel will be preached worldwide. The responsiveness of people from various ethnic groups is attested to by the experiences of people across the land.

America continues to renew itself by receiving people from throughout the world. In fact, the United States is a global mission field. Here are a few examples.

1. *Russian refugee congregation in Tennessee.*—A new Anglo church in Murfreesboro, Tennessee that meets in a school building chose to sponsor a Russian immigrant instead of getting their own building. Today there is a Russian Baptist Church in Murfreesboro.

2. *Yamile Fernandez*— Yamile, a thirteen-year-old illiterate boy in Santo Domingo, worked to support his family. An evangelistic tract someone gave him created the desire to learn to read. Unable to go to school, the youngster read everything he could get his hands on, even the classics. So strong was his desire to achieve that he came to the United States, where he worked and went to school. Eventually he earned a PhD degree. Yamile never forgot the commitment to the Lord he had made in Santo Domingo. He gave himself to planting a Hispanic church in Santa Ana, California. Yamile was attracted by the approach to church growth demonstrated by Rick

Warren, pastor of Saddleback Valley Community Church in Laguna Hills, Calif., and has gathered a congregation of 1,000 in Bible Study. The congregation meets in a rented building. Since the people are primarily laborers, they cannot pay the pastor's salary. Nor are they able to either rent a building or qualify for a loan to buy a building.

3. *Calvary Baptist Church in New Jersey.*—The Filipino and Korean mission sponsored by the Calvary Church in Aberdeen, New Jersey, started a Filipino mission with twenty-six members and a Korean mission with fifteen members.

4. *Ballard White equips Indian leaders.*—Bernie LaPlante is a young Sioux man who lives on the Cheyenne River Reservation in South Dakota. Several years ago he felt God was leading him to do more than assist his missionary pastor, Ballard White, in the church at Eagle Butte.

Bernie led out in beginning a new mission at LaPlante, a small village named for his ancestral family. For the past three years, in addition to working to provide for his family and carrying on the work at LaPlante, Bernie has been spending some time each week in a leadership training class the missionary teaches so that he will be better prepared for his ministry.

About two years ago, he became burdened for another village, Cherry Creek, which needed a church. He started visiting the village regularly. He now has services at Cherry Creek.

5. *Pastor Vang, School of Prophets.*—A Lao pastor, Brother Vang, attended a School of Prophets. There he read a Cooperative Program tract in Laotian made possible by the Woman's Missionary Union. He said, "Now that I know what the Cooperative Program is, I'm going to get my church to give 10 percent to World Missions."

6. *Vietnamese Fellowship—compiling new Vietnamese hymnal, revising the Vietnamese Bible.*—The committee elected by the Vietnamese National Fellowship came to my office to discuss their plans to compile a Vietnamese hymnal. They did not come to ask for financial help, but to request

prayer that God would provide the needed funds. Such is their faith that they are working with the Home Mission Board Marketing Department to publish the hymnal.

The love of Christ constrains Christians in America to share the gospel worldwide. Herein are some of those Southern Baptists, whose language, culture, and commitment to share the gospel have gone abroad in response to opportunities:

1. European Baptists have not forgotten their countries of origin. The Romanian Baptist Convention through its seventy-five years has worked with Baptists in Romania. In fact, a Romanian pastor, Titus Dan, serves as a foreign missionary among Romanians in Australia.

2. Hungarians in the United States, in the person of Alexander Haraszti, paved the way and have become involved with Billy Graham's efforts in Eastern Europe.

3. Eros Bacoccina, pastor of the Italian Church in San Francisco, has established work among Italians in Australia.

4. Russian and Ukrainian Baptists have, for fifty years, been supportive as well as traveled to their countries of origin to share the gospel and undergird the churches. In fact, George Boltniew, pastor in New Jersey and president of the Russian-Ukrainian Evangelical Baptist Union in the U.S.A., serves as a consultant to the Foreign Mission Board as they enter the Soviet Union. Anatolly Jaloshin, a Southern Baptist and associate director of the Russian-Ukrainian Missionary Society, serves as the liaison of Russian Baptists with the Russian-Ukrainian Convention.

5. Dan Y. Moon, at the request of the North Korean government, led fourteen Korean pastors to North Korea, where they established two churches. Later, Dan opened the way for Foreign Mission Board personnel to travel to North Korea.

6. Tommy Sohn, pastor in Dallas, spent three months in 1991 in Siberia working among Koreans.

7. The Berkland Baptist Church, in Berkeley, California,

sent its youth during the summer of 1990 to work among Koreans in Northern China.

8. The Korean Baptist Fellowship, related to the Southern Baptist Convention, has established Korean churches in eight countries in South America since 1985.

9. Hispanic pastors in the United States have led evangelistic crusades, conferences, et cetera, in Spain and in various Latin American countries.

10. The Foreign Mission Board recently began to appoint American ethnics as missionaries. Hopefully, someday, any ethnic American Southern Baptist the Lord calls to foreign missions will be able to represent the denomination.

11. American Indians representing several tribes traveled, on their own initiative and at their own expense, to Mongolia to share the gospel. There, to the surprise of the American Navajo, he discovered the ability to communicate in Mongolian. The people lived in houses similar to the hogans on the Navajo Reservation.

12. An innovative approach to missions is the plan and agreement initiated by the Foreign Mission Board of the Korea Baptist Convention and the World Mission Board of the Brazilian Baptist Convention to send missionaries to America (the nation that sends missionaries throughout the world) to evangelize ethnics in America. The approach calls for these missionaries to be assigned to the Home Mission Board of the Southern Baptist Convention. The missionaries will be appointed by both agencies. They will be assigned to, supervised by, and report to the Home Mission Board. They will receive the same benefits as other missionaries appointed by the Home Mission Board. The foreign boards will provide the funds for remuneration through the Home Mission Board.

Christian Responsibility

The heights of waves have permitted a view of the future. This view prepares us for tomorrow as the exercise of Christian responsibility gradually becoming a mode of Southern Baptist life.

Southern Baptists are becoming more responsible Christians as the consideration for witness overshadows the financial and familial (clannish) attitudes of various churches.

The University Baptist Church in Miami, Florida, owned the property of the Westland Baptist Church in Hialeah. The Hispanic congregation grew, while the Anglo congregation declined. University Baptist Church deeded the property, valued at $1.2 million, to Iglesia Bautista Westland. The Hispanic church now has an Anglo department as it seeks to minister to all persons in the community. The pastor, Andres Garcia, has led the church to self-support. At the same time, the church increased its Cooperative Program gifts by 100 percent.

First Southern Indian Baptist Church in Wichita, Kansas, is a self-supporting congregation that owns its own property. The church started a Laotian congregation in its facilities. The pastor of the Indian church resigned to pastor the Lao congregation.

A Baptist church in Phoenix voted to disband. The pastor led the church to deed the property, valued at $750,000, to the Indian Baptist Church, which became self-supporting. It has been in the top five congregations in gifts to World Missions through the Cooperative Program.

Theo Avenue Baptist Church, once a strong church in San Antonio, had declined to seven members in 1981. The group asked Efraim Diaz, a layman, for help, and encouraged him to reach Hispanics. Today the present membership exceeds 1,100. The church has been in the top fifty churches in baptisms in Texas for five consecutive years. The visitation program provides the pastor with 100 new prospects a week. The lay preacher training program sends out forty persons a week to help "weak" congregations in that part of the state.

One Southern Baptist church was led to initiate a Vietnamese congregation. The idea they had was to produce a self-supporting Vietnamese church in five years. This was based upon a statistical study, a model that had been designed for establishing and developing churches, and a policy of assisting with programs of the church for five years. The study somehow overlooked the contextual factors. Needless to say, the Vietnamese congregation has not achieved self-support. The church has responded with Christian responsibility. It has voted to continue the Vietnamese work as well as support the Cooperative Program.

Choppy Waves

There seems to be a tendency to take our eyes off the horizon of the future and look at the diminishing waves beside us. The surfer who shifts his attention toward the waves impacts his ability to maintain equilibrium and stability in motion which can result in disaster. The emerging trends toward decline are these:

1. Ethnic/language congregations are being asked to vacate the facilities of their sponsoring church. An "Anglo" pastor, whose congregation had declined, insisted that the four ethnic congregations participate in the English worship service where he preaches. The message would be interpreted. The ethnics indicated that they preferred to hear their own pastor in their own language. They were told that the "Anglo" congregation would need the use of the entire building. A date to vacate was announced.

One of the four congregations located another church building for its services and have now joined another Baptist convention. The other three are trying to find a place to meet. There have been more than fifteen such incidents in the last two years.

2. Baptist churches in two states where there are many migrants and illegals have established a new criteria for baptism. Only ethnics who are U.S. citizens are eligible for baptism.

3. Denominational entities in states with a large ethnic percentage are discouraging ethnic fellowships. They contend that, after all, this is America where everyone speaks English or will speak English. Apparently they have not read Oscar Wilde's statement, "The English have really everything in common with the Americans except, of course, the language."

4. A growing number of groups are being encouraged to use the English language lest the "Anglo" church lose members.

5. An ethnic congregation is being disbanded because it is larger than the sponsor church. The ethnics might "take over the building."

6. In several instances, ethnics are being baptized into the membership of the sponsor church. These new members are encouraged to work, attend, and tithe. However, they may not vote in business meetings.

7. Often, the sponsor insists that the offerings of the ethnic group be commingled with those of the sponsor church. The ethnic group then has to literally "beg" for stamps and other items. The sponsor church gives to world missions through the Cooperative Program; but on the records, it appears as if the ethnics do not support mission causes.

8. The implementation of unilateral policies for financial assistance seems to be an emerging trend. Some of the policies indicate that:

a. This discourages the organization of churches.

b. The ethnic pastor cannot live on the amount provided, especially since his congregation is made up of new Christians who have no idea about tithing, even if they had a job. At the end of the set time limit (five years), the congregation may seek other help, change their name and address, call on the Home Mission Board, or as a last resort, either join another denomination or just fade away.

9. There have been instances where local leaders have encouraged the sponsor church, which is in transition and

decline, to sell its building to another denomination rather than sell or give it to the ethnic group who really kept the sponsor church alive. The ethnics become "Christian nomads."

10. Insensitivity in providing equipping and participatory opportunities—because such calls for extra effort in preparation and implementation—is gradually driving ethnic groups to become involved with independent groups and/or to secure language materials and leadership somewhere else.

The last part of the twentieth century has brought about a change in American attitudes toward ethnicity. Ethnic pride, identity, and retention of language and culture values have created the American mosaic in which colorful, individual pieces are fitted together to describe the lives of Americans who live on the edge of tomorrow.

Barriers to Future Growth

In the midst of the responsiveness of ethnic people to the gospel, emerging trends are becoming barriers to ethnic church growth. In a sense, it is a speck in our vision. These are viable concerns that have shown up in various settings.

1. Everybody should speak English, besides "we are all alike;" we don't need a language congregation.

2. The director of missions in an urban city insisted that no new work be started during the Laser Thrust. New work could only be started if it had been planned by the association.

3. The discouraging of ethnic missions being organized into churches, lest "they" become more in number than "us."

4. Guidelines that become policies and later determine whether or not a new ethnic work or church can be planted. They don't have a sponsor. A mission can't sponsor new work; can't be admitted into the association since they don't own property, et cetera.

5. Cost effective missions—the unwillingness to plant new ethnic churches because they cannot become self-supporting immediately, and their contributions to missions are small.

6. Sponsor churches that smother aggressive ethnic congregations—often it has been said, "They need to be Americans like us."

7. The recognition, encouragement, and support of Anglo churches that "split" doctrinally from the associations; yet neglecting to acknowledge and support ethnic fellowships that organize, by the book, into an association.

Pogo once said, "We has met the enemy, and it is us."

Challenge for Southern Baptists

Time is affecting the height, velocity, and direction of ethnic work as Southern Baptists ride the crest of the wave. In the United States the church is approaching the twenty-first century with a nineteenth-century institutional structure. The changing global demographics will impact the changing racial and ethnic composition of the nation. The 1990s provide Southern Baptists an opportunity to prepare for the flourishing twenty-first century.

William Faulkner once said, "The church will not be destroyed by those on the outside, nor those on the inside, but by the professional religionist who will take the bells out of the steeple." Mesmerized by theories and statistics, many of the socioreligionists have lost touch with the grass-roots vitality of America.[3]

Southern Baptists are faced with the most complex challenge in the history of Christianity as efforts are made to share the gospel contextually with ethnics in America. "The teeming multitudes of all colors, languages, smells, and cultures are not just a quaint sideline in our nation."[4] Less than 4 percent of Americans who identify themselves with a language and culture other than English have had a personal experience with Jesus Christ.

1. Segmentation of America's Mission Field—People desire to be seen as a particular type of person; people are proud of

their achievements as well as their cultural and linguistic heritage. The social fabric of the nation is changing.

2. Planting and Developing of Contextual Churches—The old neighborhood is becoming a cultural community; a community whose cohesiveness is not only professional, but cultural and linguistic as well. Ethnic church planting will need to move beyond "just planting" and include cultivating, developing, and harvesting. The ethnic churches are today where Southern Baptists were fifty to seventy-five years ago. The ethnic church is now the Southern Baptist church of the future.

The responsiveness of ethnic people to the gospel calls for long-range "blue-chip" investments rather than "cost-effective penny stock." Phase-down programs should be in light of the context of each congregation instead of a "rule of thumb," unless the harvest be premature.

3. Contextual Methodology—The ethnic diversity calls for different methods that are applicable to the targeted group. It is already evident that the present methodology is irrelevant to various segments of the denomination, not just ethnics. Although it may seem financially unprofitable and almost humanly impossible, methods relevant to the various segments— ethnic, racial, rural, urban—must be developed lest these methods are sought from other groups.

Materials designed (not translated nor adapted) to meet the needs of the people (as perceived by those people), and produced in their own language are essential. The affordability of these materials will determine whether or not these groups become a vibrant part of the denomination.

4. Shared Leadership—Traditionally, leaders have come from a particular section of the country, been influenced by certain institutions, and have been "lily white." There have been four exceptions. Serious consideration should be given to sharing leadership among Anglo, African-American and ethnic leaders.

Active and equal participation (not involvement) by aggressive ethnic leaders will become the glue that binds the cohesiveness of the denomination. The current infrastructures will need to be reexamined and altered if ethnic Southern Baptists are to be a viable part of the denomination. Experience and education indicate a person identified with and by the people can be, in fact is, more effective. Future leaders must be equipped.

5. American Ethnics—People born and educated in the United States are proud of their heritage. These people often prefer the use of American English; yet their cohesiveness is their inherited culture. English-speaking ethnic churches should be aggressively planted to meet the spiritual needs of this segment of Americans.

6. Missionaries from Abroad—Christians in other nations are concerned for their friends and relatives who reside in the United States and for their spiritual welfare. Baptists in Korea and Brazil will send missionaries to America who will serve and work as a part of the Home Mission Board's missionary endeavors. World missions will begin with the evangelization of America.

7. Urban America— The potential for failure is being built into the planning if the growth potential of those who live and work among the ethnic and racial core of urban America is overlooked. These ethnic and black leaders have already forgotten more about urban areas than demographers and planners will ever learn about urban Americans. Ethnics and blacks comprise the heart of the cities and live and work among the people.

8. Ethnic Fellowships—Although ethnic associations have existed since 1842, three years prior to the organization of the Southern Baptist Convention, there is a tendency to negate their existence. Socioreligious fellowships exist in the denomination in various forms, locations, and so forth.

People come together naturally whether encouraged or discouraged. Baptists should explore the participatory involvement of these in the life of the denomination. The assertiveness, cohesiveness, and commitment of ethnic Southern Baptists will accelerate.

9. Growth Measurement—Church Growth Holography is the three-dimensional measurement related to ethnic church growth. These dimensions are cultural, contextual, and numerical.

10. North American Marketing—The entire industrial geography of North America is going to change.

People are coming to America. Baptists must be ready and committed to evangelize global America. Demosthenes, in 343 B.C., stated, "Small opportunities are often the beginning of great enterprises."

Ninth Wave

There is an ancient superstition of the sea that, inevitably, one wave is greater than any that has preceded it. It is called the Ninth Wave. It is the power culmination of sea and wind. There is no greater force. To catch the Ninth Wave we must hone our skills and improve our timing.

The Ninth Wave, propelled by languages and cultures, is approaching America. Here are some trends that seem to indicate that our nation is about to be engulfed and reshaped.

1. *The American mosaic will intensify.*—The world's birthrate, as predicted in *The Global 2000 Report to the President,* will impact the nation. There is a possibility that at least 30 percent of the births in the Third World countries will seek to migrate to the United States. The Hong Kong Treaty of 1997 is already bringing thousands to our shores. A recent ruling permits persons who invest a million dollars in the United States to enter the country as immigrants. The Pacific Rim nations will, in all probability, increase immigration by 10 percent to 20 percent.

2. *The economy will impact the ethnic "harder."*—The twentieth-century triad (the United States, Asia, and Europe)

trade agreements will dilute jobs. The North American free-trade market (the United States, Canada, and Mexico), although designed to move goods across borders, will contribute to unemployment as well as employment, especially along the Mexican border.

3. *Foreign investments will bring more people and more employment.*—Foreign investments will provide opportunities for Americans, formerly employed by American-owned corporations, to be employed by foreign-owned corporations.

4. *The military will be predominately ethnic.*—It is estimated that in excess of 50 percent of the armed forces will be Hispanic, with other ethnic groups contributing an additional 10 to 20 percent.

5. *Immigration is essential to the nation.*—The Census Bureau estimates that without immigration the population growth of the United States will begin to decline early in the next century.

6. *Ethnic birth rates will increase.*—Ethnic births in the United States are already higher than Anglo (European) birth rates.

7. *Schools, various states, and so forth, as a result of pressure groups, will focus on the use of the American English language.*—The use of various languages in the homes will intensify. Today over 150 languages are used by children in schools. If equal justice is to be provided, then the courts will need personnel who speak a language other than American English. The police in major cities, such as Los Angeles, communicate in forty-two languages to enforce the law.

8. *Old neighborhoods will vanish as cultural communities emerge.*—Yuppie communities have joined the ethnic cultural communities. The church, if it is to survive, will need to give attention to cultural and linguistic segmentation; thus permitting people to become Christians without having to cross cultural and linguistic barriers.

9. *The American ethnic will increasingly impact the Ameri-*

can way of life.—Already there is a significant number of political and governmental leaders from among the invisible American ethnic who serve in places of influence. Visible ethnics, denoted by their features, will increasingly seek and secure leadership in numerous areas of influence. American ethnic leaders will replace the "old" traditional leaders.

10. *International mobility will impact the globalization of the gospel.*—The evangelization of ethnics in America will "constrain" them to share the gospel with their relatives in their country of origin. These will be natural leaders equipped by birth to speak a language other than American English, understand the culture, be able to live among the people, and so forth. This is already taking place. The development of the common markets, the triad, et cetera, will lead to a borderless world that permits international mobility.

11. *The number of religions practiced in the United States will increase.*—Today there are Muslim, Buddhist, and Hindu temples in every major city. Christian churches have fled the inner city and sold their facilities to a variety of religious groups. The military currently appoints Buddhist chaplains. People migrating to the United States will bring religious beliefs that many Americans did not know existed.

These are some of the trends that will impact the future of our nation. Hopefully, the sharing of these will help the church to accomplish the Great Commission to proclaim the biblical message to those who are a part of the American mosaic.

The waves of time continually erode the beach, grind the mighty boulders, and shape people's lives. One may be able to control erosion, but only God can shape one's eternal destination. Christians, in response to the Great Commission, can seriously view the trends as guides for leading people everywhere to acquire eternal life.

Notes

1. Theodore Mall, "Asian Indians in America" (Atlanta: Home Mission Board, 1985), unpublished paper.

2. Kenichi Ohmae, *The Borderless World; Power and Strategy in the Interlinked Economy* (New York: McKinney and Co., Inc., 1990), 21.

3. Austin H. Kiplinger and Knight A. Kiplinger, *America in the Global 90s* (Washington, D.C.: Kiplinger Books, 1989), 4.

4. C. Peter Wagner, "A Vision for Evangelizing the Real America" *International Bulletin of Missionary Research,* April, 1986, 61.